born in sin

evelyn coleman

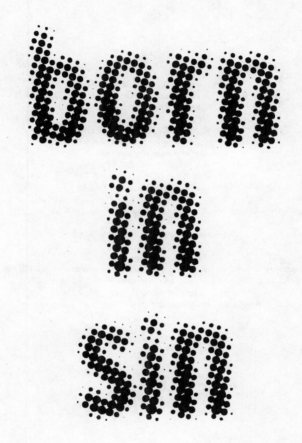

born in sin

A RICHARD JACKSON BOOK
ATHENEUM BOOKS FOR YOUNG READERS
NEW YORK • LONDON • TORONTO • SYDNEY • SINGAPORE

16⁰⁰

Athenuem Books for Young Readers
An imprint of Simon & Schuster Children's Publishing Division
1230 Avenue of the Americas
New York, New York 10020
Copyright © 2001 by Evelyn Coleman
Book design by Angela Carlino
The text of this book is set in Janson Text.
Printed in the United States of America
2 4 6 8 10 9 7 5 3 1
Library of Congress Cataloging-in-Publication Data
Coleman, Eveyln, 1948–
Born in sin / by Evelyn Coleman.—1st ed.
    p.   cm.
"A Richard Jackson book"
Summary: Despite serious obstacles and setbacks, fourteen-year-old Keisha
pursues her dream of becoming an Olympic swimmer and medical doctor.
ISBN 0-689-83833-6
1. Afro-Americans—Juvenile fiction. [1. Afro-Americans—
Fiction. 2. Swimming—Fiction.]
I. Title.
PZ7.C6746 Bo 2001
[Fic]—dc21   00-025947

FIRST EDITION

To

Laverne Young, a gifted swimmer

*Tommy Jackson, head coach of Atlanta
Dolphins Swim Team*

*Charles Candy, assistant coach of Atlanta
Dolphins Swim Team*

*The gracious staff of Georgia Hill,
Atlanta-Fulton Public Library*

May the force always be with you!

And to

*Dick Jackson, a man of great
vision and courage*

My mama say, "Things either gonna get better or get worse round this house." Sounds crazy, don't it? Mama say stuff like that sometimes, and we just bust out laughing. She a good mama, though. She cleans up at a motel. She don't report her money or nothin' but she got her reasons. If she do report it, she say, "Then y'all won't have no deodorant, no toilet tissue, no washing powder, no soap, no nothing. The welfare people might be worried 'bout you eatin', but yo' mama is worrying about you stinkin'." See, she be jone-ing.

She, my mama, Carolyn Wright, sleeps in the day 'cause she has to get up early. She gotta be at work by

4:00 a.m. in the morning. So you know that's why she ain't there to wake you up like they do on TV for you to go to school. She don' told you what to do if you smell smoke, see flames, or hear somebody breaking down the door. "You grab your brother and sister and the baby, and haul your ass out the window. You hear gunfire, you drop to the floor." That simple.

"Keisha Wright," she says, "when you get up in the morning, you gon' have to get your little brother ready."

So when you gets up, Punky's yelling and screaming like a fool, 'cause he ain't got good sense. And you doing all you can do to get him to shut up and get dressed. Then you got to find him something to eat. You know it gon' be cereal and other times it gon' be toast and butter. Every now and then it's some leftover food from the night before. And sometimes y'all ain't got no milk, so you be putting together cereal and water. But he don't care 'cause he too busy fussing and whining his little behind off.

Your big sister, Rhenda, who ain't but seventeen, ain't no help 'cause she 'sleep. But it's 'cause Tomika, her two-year-old baby, who was born a preemie and is not as big as other kids, don' been crying all night and kept her up. It's all right with you, though. Your sister quit school 'cause she don't want no stranger keeping her baby. God, she love that baby.

At home you just chillin'. Here, everybody you know is sitting on the stoop. Ain't nobody got nothing you ain't got. You want fingernails done, hair braided, Nikes, FUBU, you know if you beg long enough, and wait long enough, your mama gon' get it for you. She gonna fuss and say you 'bout to break her or send her to the po'-house. You know she got that po'house stuff from your grandma 'cause ain't no such thing. But she gon' say it, anyway, like it could happen. And she gon' yell, "You must be crazy to keep asking me for stuff." Then she gon' just swear up and down she ain't got no money.

But you also know she definitely gonna be grinning when she see you struttin' round in whatever she don' bought you. And she gon' be bragging to her friends how good her kids is looking.

It don't matter that you don't always have meat to eat, even though bacon is like your favorite thing. You could eat a whole pack of bacon at one time—if you had it. You dreaming half the time you lived on a pig farm.

Sometimes—especially when your mama gets a new man, which ain't that often, and she's trying to act like she cook all the time—you as happy as she is. 'Cause then y'all gon' have bacon, eggs, and grits for breakfast when he comes over. Mama ain't gon' let him spend the night, not with Rhenda and me there, but he can come to eat in the morning. And on Sunday you gon' have a sho'nuf meal. 'Cause her new man is trying to show off and act like he could be a good daddy and don' bought some groceries.

You have pizza sometimes, too. And that's great 'cause you can use that the next morning to get Punky to act better. Leftover pizza is what *he* love. You don't care that the pizza man don't deliver to your neighborhood 'cause he scared. You just think he scared 'cause he's white and ain't no whites living in public housing where you at.

All you know is you here. You ain't really that scared

unless somebody is shooting, which is not all the time. And by the time they mostly shooting, you got to be in the house in the bed, anyway, 'cause your mama say you ain't gon' be fast and hang out.

But then everything changes. You start thinking maybe something ain't right, something is wrong with you, 'cause somebody else who can't stand to see you smiling and eating no ice cream gon' try to melt it for you. That's what happened to me. One day just before summer vacation when I was going to the tenth grade it happened to me.

I think I was pretty happy until that day. Maybe not totally jump up and down, spin around kinda happy, but I wasn't crying all the time, neither. Naw. That's 'cause then, when I was fourteen, I didn't know no better. See, I didn't get it. Even after Ms. Hill call me in her guidance counselor office the week before, I didn't get it. She asked me straight-faced and all, "Miss Keisha, didn't I see you rapping last year in one of the assembly programs?"

"Yeah," I say, thinking she saying it 'cause she proud of me. "My brother Punky, he wrote it. He's real good." I sat up, smiling at her.

"Then you want to be a rapper, right?"

I shifted. Felt squirmy inside and said, "Nooooo."

"A singer, then?"

"Noooo. I don't want to be no rapper or a singer. I *was* rapping last year, but I'm fourteen now."

She smiled sweet, like she'd been sucking sour candy. "So, what do people do different in the music business when they get fourteen, then?"

I shifted in the chair. "I don't know what they do," I said, pursing my lips.

"What about basketball? You're tall; did you play at middle school?"

"Yes, I played. They say I was pretty good. But"—I shrugged—"I'm not planning on playing no basketball for a living, either."

"Surely you're not thinking about quitting school? Even though you *can* get your GED after you're eighteen here in Georgia."

My face got hot. "Don't you have my records?" I asked her. "I'm making straight A's. I ain't fooling around no more. I want to go to medical school."

"Uh-huh," she said, flipping through my records on her desk. Then she stood up. A grown person's signal that they through with you, like you some rotten food don' landed in they lap.

"I think it's good that a girl like you has dreams, Keisha. Real good. Just keep holding your head up."

I heard what she was saying, but I didn't understand. But I remember that I felt funny about it, and dropped my head. I still didn't get it. All I knew was for some reason I didn't feel like looking up into her muddy, light brown eyes. They always reminded me of tea with milk in it. Me and Rhenda call that skeleton tea. Not that we'd tasted a skeleton or nothin', but it just seem like a skeleton might taste like that tea. We both hate it. Now when I think about skeletons I think about Ms. Hill and not that tea no more. 'Cause skeletons ain't got no heart. They ain't really human. Yep. Ms. Hill and skeletons—

'bout the same. But you know what? I still didn't get it. How would I know that there's things people can do and say that's just as bad as if they cursed you out and slapped you upside the head? And they doing it all just to help.

In homeroom, like always, the crackling started first. "Will the following Primm students please report to the office: Keisha Wright, Betty Shabazz, Kente Shabazz, Malik Shabazz, Roberta Santos, Elayna Rodriguez, Paulie Cooper, and Sammy Ray Lee."

I'm thinking, Why they got to say Primm students? They think other school's students here?

I heard a *pssst*.

I turned around and looked into the face of a goat.

"Keisha Wright, you in trouble."

"Kiss my you-know-what, Sammy Ray," I said. "I ain't in no trouble." But I wasn't as sure as I sounded.

Why would *anybody* call me to the office with Sammy Ray goat-head Lee? He *stayed* in trouble. I ain't been in no real trouble since I was nine years old and I pushed Jackie Payton out of the swing 'cause she called me a punk. And I quit talking in class this year. I was trying to think what they could be calling me for while I got my books together.

Ms. Parker, my homeroom teacher, looked at me and barked, "Take all your things with you, Keisha. You're not coming back today."

"Why ain't I?" I asked her.

"How many times do I have to tell you it's not 'Why ain't I?' Just get your things and go to the office like-I-said."

She hates me, Ms. Parker. She hates me and I don't know why. I'm the only black girl in her class and she's black, too. Real black. Blacker than me, even. But she just plain hates me. Ever since I got to ninth grade she's been picking on me about something. "Good," I said to her. "I'm glad to not come back." I rolled my eyes to let her know she ain't the only one who can hate somebody.

I yanked my book bag out from under my desk and stuffed my books inside. Sammy Ray had already gone. He was a white boy, but she didn't hate him. He was the biggest troublemaker in school and most times Ms. Parker act like he ain't doing or saying nothing. At least that part was right—he wasn't doing nothing. And he never had any books with him, so it was easy for *him* to leave.

"Do you have to disrupt the entire class just to get your books, Keisha?"

I wanted to say, Yes, yes I do, but I didn't. I wasn't talking to that witch no more today. All she wanted was for me to be in trouble. Naw. It ain't gonna happen. That would make her way too happy.

I tiptoed to the door, looked back at her, and smiled. Then I walked out in the hall, sat my book bag down on the floor, and slammed the door shut as hard as I could. *That* ought to help her.

On my way to the office my heartbeat speeded up. I realized I knew what this was about—why I was called to the office. I applied for the special summer program for smart kids. I been making straight A's and B's since I was in the third grade. Last year I made up my mind to become a doctor. I was even let into the tenth grade chemistry class this semester.

I picked up my feet higher. I felt lighter, like maybe I was gonna float right through the ceiling. Man. This was the bomb—that means something good getting ready to blow up for you. I stopped and straightened my blouse and tucked it inside my skirt. Dag. I hated our iron was broke. I wanted to look nice when Ms. Hill told me in front of the other kids they called that I was there for something else.

It had to be that I'd been selected. That had to be it. I shot into the bathroom and combed my hair. My hair was the longest it had ever been and I was glad. I loved having long hair. Rhenda had long hair and so did Mama, down their backs. But mine never grew that long. Grandma used to put black thread on it and hook the plaits together to make my hair grow. Mama buys me special grease now.

I suppose it's working—a little, I said, looking at it in the mirror. The edges were kinky, but when it's getting hot out, ain't no helping that.

I attempted to pull some of the wrinkles out of my blouse by smoothing out the cloth with my hands. It didn't work. This blouse was made from permanent-wrinkle material. I looked at myself again. My pug nose stuck out on my face. My mama said my kind of nose runs in the family. "People," my mama say, "can look and see that you come from healthy people who don't have no problem with breathing when it's hot." She says stuff like that to me and Rhenda—you know, to make us feel good about how we look. We both dark chocolate girls. When we was little and kids be picking on us, we'd run home and tell Mama. We would say, "So and so callin' us black."

Mama just squinch up her face, lean back with one hand on her hip, and say, "So. You *are* black. What? You don't like looking like me? Besides, the blacker the berry the sweeter the juice." For a while she almost make me stop *eating* berries.

Mama liked for me to feel good about myself and she liked me doing good in school. She said she was proud of my grades when I brought my last report card home. She say, "Smart girls don't make dumb mistakes." I know what she really talking about. Getting pregnant.

This summer I was gonna go to college, Avery University—a rich folk's college with a medical school and all. Can you believe it? They were doing a special program for the smart kids who wanted to be in medicine.

The summer was for the orientation. Then in the fall we start a three-year program that would allow us special admission to Avery after we graduate high school.

We are going to be bused there every day because the university is a long ways away. We're going to have lunch in the cafeteria, free. Every kid gets a computer of his or her own to take home.

I walked faster now, psyched up about hearing the announcement. I was more excited than I'd ever been. Hey, this was gonna be the best summer of my life.

When I got to the office the secretary told me everyone needed to go in the classroom next door. She said there wasn't enough room in the office for the meeting.

"What kind of meeting?" I asked her, thinking to myself, This don't seem right. I figured them other kids called to the office was in trouble, and ain't had nothing to do with me. The secretary grunted and pointed toward the door. When I got in the room the other kids were already there, sitting down. A man and a woman that I'd never seen before sat up front with Ms. Hill. She was looking through some papers. The kids she'd called, on the same list as me, were acting silly, along with a few kids I didn't know. They were all making too much noise, including Sammy Ray Lee.

I sat down and said, "Shut up, y'all, so she can talk. You know Ms. Hill don't like no talking when she talking." If she was giving us a standardized test the crazy woman would just stand up front, rolling her eyes around till everyone in the room stop breathing, just so she go ahead and stop making them ugly faces. Everybody was still yapping, so I added, "And you know she ain't gon' talk till we quiet." I actually knew better English, but if I'd used it they woulda' never shut up.

"*You* shut up, turd brain," Kente Shabazz said loudly.

"Leave her alone," Betty said, her pencil whipping through the air at his head.

She was named after Dr. Betty Shabazz—but she don't act like she even know who that was.

"Don't be taking up for her, fool," Malik Shabazz shouted. "She coming down on your own brother."

Then they started fussing real loud with each other. All three of them were half brothers and sister. They were all in the same grade 'cause Malik and Kente had been left back. Betty was in her right grade, tenth going on to eleventh. She could still be mean if she wanted to. Me and her weren't no best friends, even though we were in the same PE class, where some of the ninth grade is in with the tenth, so I think she just was taking up for me to get back at them.

Then Ms. Hill looked up and said, "Children, please be quiet."

I smiled. Ms. Hill was one of those black people who act entirely different when any bigwig folks around. I knew that the two people must be real special company from Avery 'cause otherwise she'd be yelling, "You better sit your little behinds down before I throw *all y'all* out."

Malik was still talking and I waited for her to ask him to step out in the hall but she didn't. Instead, she began telling us about our lives.

Ms. Hill say in her excited voice she's got a "wonderful opportunity for at-risk children." She says this to us just like we been knowing full well, all the time, we at-risk of something. Until that moment I don't know what she even talking about.

I swung my head around, looking to see if the others knew what she meant. I was the smartest kid in there, and I didn't know, so I figured we were all lost. But something in her way of saying this silenced everybody, even Malik. He was looking at his feet, slumped down in the chair so far, I thought if he wasn't so big he'd slip right under the desk arm.

The way Ms. Hill kept talking soon made me want to cry. For a minute I couldn't even hear her no more. I could just hear the sound of what she was saying but not the words. She sound like she talking about some ants who don' showed up uninvited to her picnic.

It turned out Sammy Ray Lee was the only one who really understood her. He jumped up out of his seat and shouted, "Wait a minute. You old witch, how you know what we got? I'm outta here. You ain't nothin', either," and he stormed out.

The two visitors looked stunned. Then they went back to shaking their heads in agreement that me and the other kids was at-risk for something. Not just any old something, but something really bad.

Ms. Hill kept saying to us in such a sweet, helping voice, "This program will enable you to live a better life. You'll be surrounded by educated people, people who care about what happens to you. People who can help you learn to live right and do the right things."

Now I was really confused. Weren't the teachers doing all this? Weren't they educated?

Ms. Hill kept on talking, raising her voice higher, like she was getting all worked up. She said if these people didn't help us, we were not just going to have bad luck, we were going to use or sell crack, have no self-esteem, no self-respect, be killing each other or go to jail—and that there wasn't much we could do about the future unless somebody, like them, saved us from how we lived.

To me, how I lived meant living with my mama, my sister and Tomika, and my brother. I lived with my family.

Ms. Hill continued loudly, in a TV preacher's voice, "Unless you attend this program, there isn't much hope for you." And then she warned us, "I know if no one else can see it, one day you all are going to be dead."

I thought to myself, even though I didn't really curse that often, What in the hell she talking about? Everybody gonna be dead one day.

Then the man got up. He told us how happy he was to see us. And the woman said she was going to pass out this paper for our *mamas* to sign so we could have permission to attend their special summer program.

I thought, *mamas?* Some of us got daddies, you know. Not me, of course, but still—I didn't say nothing. Our daddy is dead. I just took the paper she handed me and looked for that blue emblem I remembered on top of all the forms I had filled out that said AVERY UNIVERSITY. But it wasn't there. Wasn't nothing there to tell you where the paper come from. Nothing but a place to fill in your name and stuff. And some kind of government-funding crap. So I raised my hand.

Ms. Hill looked up at me and said, "Yes, Keisha darling."

I squeezed up my face. *Yes, Keisha darling?* When did she ever call us anything like that? Man, was she showing out.

"Ms. Hill," I said, clearing my throat and trying to think proper English in my head. My mama say you got to be bilingual if you want to get a good job one day. She say it's all right to talk however you want to at home, but don't do it at school. "Excuse me, but is this the permission form for my mother to fill out for Avery? Because Ms. Oliver, you know Ms. Dorothy Oliver, said the other day she spoke to the director and he said I was already in, even though I hadn't finished the interview process. I mean, I've been preliminarily accepted to the program. All that was left was for me to be notified about my interview time. And my mother to fill out the permission form."

"First of all," Ms. Hill said, smiling at me from behind the desk, "Ms. Oliver is a biology teacher, not a guidance counselor, and she shouldn't have been messing with that."

"Yes, but she was helping me with—"

"It's okay. She didn't know your history. It's important to be practical about our expectations in making choices. I'm sorry, Keisha, that she mislead you. But I changed your curriculum from college prep to general for the next school term. You aren't eligible for that program anymore. This is the program you got—I mean, the program you were assigned to. I feel this one will be better for you in the long run. It's a special program for at-risk kids."

Now I could see what I didn't notice before: Ms. Oliver is black and she cares about me, but Ms. Hill is just like Ms. Parker: She might be black, but she hates me, too. I took a deep, long breath and said, "You know what, Ms. Hill. Ain't the hospital just a few blocks away?"

"Why yes, Keisha, it is a few blocks away. But this program is not at the hospital."

"I know that. But I ain't the one at risk. You are." And I leaped over the desk to get to her.

I grabbed for Ms. Hill and yanked her blouse toward
me. A few buttons flew off. I needed to get to her head. My
fingers curled around her long, hay-looking hair and I
snatched my hand back triumphant. Not only did I have her
hair but her brown stocking cap with a knot tied in the end
of it. Her hair (her real hair, that is) was in little black plaits
sticking up on her head like Eddie Murphy's Buckwheat.

Ms. Hill grabbed her head and screamed like a loony
cutting loose in the woods.

I swung her fake hair over my head in a circle and
jumped up and down, laughing.

Malik was stomping on top of the desk, laughing

so hard, tears was rolling down his face. "Damn," he rapped, "she ain't got no hair hardly at all. She be needing a new hair fall, and man, she be short not tall."

Betty yelled, "And that shit is napppppeeee. God, we thinking she got good hair up in here and look what's under that rag?"

Ms. Hill stumbled, tripped, and raced from the room, yelling for Mr. Bassgate the principal to call the police.

The two white people ain't even moved a muscle. They staring—no, glaring at me, all big-eyed like I'm gonna get them next.

I stepped toward them to say, "I'm sorry."

But they threw up their arms to cover their face and head.

They didn't know nothin' 'bout me—I ain't gon' hit nobody. And besides, they ain't got no wigs on. I stepped back and didn't say nothing else. What was the use?

I heard Mr. Bassgate running down the hall, swearing like he was in a pool room.

Ms. Hill was barking out stuff like a freaking wild dog right behind him.

The school security guy ran with them through the door.

Mr. Simms, the security guy who's too stupid to even be working near a school let alone in one, grabs my arm. "Girl, you don' don' it now."

I snatched my arm from him and said, "You better take your stinkin' hands *off* me."

He pulled out a stick and lifted it up like he was gon' hit me.

Malik dived off the desk.

He and Simms crashed to the floor. They rolled around, knocking over desks and cursing at each other.

I didn't move 'cause this wasn't what I wanted to happen. I didn't want no fighting. I attempted to pull them off each other.

Mr. Bassgate grabbed me by the hair and yanked me up.

I screamed and tried to get him off me, but when I was turning around my elbow jabbed him in the face.

He swore loudly and shoved me.

I stumbled forward and hit my mouth on the corner of a chair. Blood shot out like a bullet from a gun and splashed on the white woman's face.

She screamed so loud, everybody just stopped, motionless.

I looked up to see if somehow she'd been shot for real.

She was screaming and jumping up and down.

The white man was patting her shoulder and talking to her soft-like.

Betty was still laughing.

The other kids were hooting like fools.

Sirens screeched in the background while I held my mouth with my hand.

Malik was sitting on Simms now, smoking a cigarette that he wasn't supposed to have in school.

And Ms. Hill, who had picked her wig up off the floor, was still crying like an idiot with it sitting up on her head crooked. Her makeup looked like she belonged on a TV preaching show. You know, the ones where they got all that gold furniture in the back of 'em.

Police rushed through the door as if there was a bank robbery going down. And they grabbed me up like I'd been the one stealing the money.

Two other cops dragged Malik off that ignoramus Simms. They twisted Malik's arm behind his back and made him lay facedown on the floor.

Malik still held his cigarette in his mouth. But now it was crushed 'cause they don' smashed his head hard on the floor two times that I could count.

I was mad for real now 'cause that wasn't necessary, and Malik hadn't really done nothing to deserve it. They tied these plastic things around his wrist and then yanked him up to his feet. Now his face was bloody too.

A policewoman tied the plastic things around my wrists.

Ms. Hill was yelling that they got to take me to jail 'cause I threatened to kill her.

The lying witch.

The white man, who had been acting like he'd only had a bit part in this movie, said to the cops, "Look, this is a misunderstanding. There is no need to take these young people to jail. We're here to help them. They don't understand any other way to resolve conflict." Then, he turned to the police-uniformed brother who seemed to be in charge. "Are you in charge, sir?"

The brother cop said, "Yeah. I'm in charge." Then, like he'd just now figured out that he ought to be proud about it, he stuck out his chest and repeated, "Yeah, man. I'm the one in charge."

"Well sir, I'm attorney Carl Pierce. We're with the Save the Children At-Risk Foundation, SCARF. We came here to help these unfortunate young people, not get them in trouble. So hopefully we can resolve this misunderstanding in a civilized and peaceful manner. We're enrolling your young people in a program that will help them with all their emotional problems. Surely as an African American you can understand that these children have no resources, no values, and no home training and that's why the last thing they need is to be carted off to jail to comingle with *more* criminals. They need to get out of this neighborhood and see how responsible citizens live. Do you understand what I'm trying to say here?"

"Yes, I do," the brother said. He nodded to his men, and they began snapping off my plastic cuffs.

One of them asked the brother-in-charge, "What about this one, sir," and pointed to Malik. "You don't mean him, do you?"

"No. We're taking him with us."

I shouted, "No. I'm the one who started this. He was just trying to help me. Please. Please don't do that." I felt like a snake. No, lower than a snake.

The white man, Mr. Pierce, continued, "Sir, I'll take the boy into my custody and I assure you this will not happen again. You realize your young men are statistically at risk even more than your young women. Just let us have him. We will help him learn better problem solving and conflict resolution skills. Our program will teach him the importance of taking care of his children. We will even go pick up his children so he can spend quality time with them under our supervision. What do you say?"

"Hmm. Where's the program?" the brother police asked.

"In Fountainhead. Believe me, when we bring these kids back here, no one will recognize them. We plan to transform them into good and honest people—responsible people."

I thought, Ain't nobody stupid here. I knew this black policeman heard what this white man was really saying. I knew he lived in this neighborhood 'cause I knew one of his kids. He got to know. He really talking 'bout you, too, brother. I waited. This brother was probably gon' take that night stick and knock him in the head. Plus, Malik ain't even got no children.

The brother looked at the white man and smiled. "Okay. You got a deal." He nodded to the two cops holding Malik, and they snipped off his plastic and pushed him forward.

Malik was back to looking down at the floor.

Mr. Pierce put his hand lightly on Malik's shoulder.

Malik jerked away and picked up one of the desks with one hand, turned it up, and sat in it.

I figured me and Malik were the only ones who really knew what the white man was saying 'bout us. And we may have been the only ones who cared. 'Cause now all the other kids was jumping round the white man, asking him, "Is he gon' have good food when we come to his program?"

Me, I ain't asking him shit. I see right now going to Fountainhead ain't about nothing. They sho'nuf be trippin'.

Ms. Hill was busy yelling that we were getting off too easy and she wanted to press charges.

I gathered up my books and walked out the door.

Mr. Bassgate was saying, "Keisha, you ain't getting your grades till your mama comes up here for them. You've got some punishment coming your way, young lady."

I didn't care what he was saying. I left. And, I didn't look back to see if the white man or the police or anybody else was coming after me. All I wanted was to go home to my mama.

On the way home I thought about Malik. I didn't want to. He's just a dumb old boy. I try not to go crazy thinking about boys. It's enough girls thinking 'bout boys without me doing it, too. I got plans. Big plans. And right now ain't no boys in them. But I thought about him, anyway. About him taking up for me like that. Finally, I said to myself, Keisha, he too weird to think about. Then I put him out of my mind.

Mama, she wasn't mad at me after I told her what happened. She don' taught me I got to stand up for myself no matter what. I know some people think black people don't do nothing but fight, shoot, and kill somebody. But that ain't so. I ain't never hit nobody, unless you count my little brother, when my mama ain't home, and he won't mind. Or the one time me and Rhenda went at it. I didn't like it then and I don't like fighting now. I wasn't gonna hit Ms. Hill, that old heifer, as my grandma used to call people like her. But one thing I knew about black women whether they was rich or poor. They don't want nobody messing with their hair even if they don' bought it from a store.

So I already knew if I pulled Ms. Hill's wig off, then she was gon' leave me alone and start that screaming just like she did.

I told Mama the principal said she was gonna have to come to school before I could get my grades. But then they musta thought my mama was gonna raise hell 'cause they called that same evening and said she ain't got to come, they gon' mail the grades home. I didn't care what they was gon' do as long as I got them. I was going to submit my own forms to Avery.

I didn't like the thought of going to the at-risk group, but Mama say, "Girl, it ain't gon' hurt you to try it. You ain't lazing round here all summer, that's for sure. Hey, if life throws you a curve, you better ride it."

Mama so funny. She'll twist some saying around in a hot minute.

Monday morning I was standing outside waiting for them at-risk people to drive us to some community center in Fountainhead when Jeebie stopped by my stoop. Jeebie's a drug dealer. Some people call him a drug lord. My mama say, "Ain't no damn drug dealer should be called no Lord."

Jeebie said, "Hey, little sister." He spun his toothpick round with his tongue. "You wanna make some quick money this summer?"

'Bout that time, Mr. Hakim, a man near the same age as Jeebie, popped up from nowhere. He musta' been standing near Jeebie's car parked across the street. "No man. Don't mess with her. Okay? She is one of the smart girls around here. Leave her be, man."

"Hey, Keem. I needs me some smart girl runners, too, man. What up wid you?"

"I said, leave her be," Mr. Hakim said, fierce enough to make a bee stop buzzing.

I ain't saying nothing, like my mama told me. I'm studying the sidewalk and wishing they would both disappear. I didn't know either one of them that well. But I was glad Mr. Hakim showed up for sure. I didn't know his last name. Everybody just called him Mr. Hakim. He ran some kind of center for wayward teens or something like that.

"Let's go, man. Come on," Mr. Hakim said.

I could see their shadow, and Mr. Hakim had Jeebie by the arm.

"Yo, man. I don' told you 'bout encouraging this white man shit. This girl family got to live. Got to eat. I got as much right to be talking to Carolyn's kids as you have. Why you trippin' on me?"

"And I told you, the white man didn't invent learning. Africans began civilization, my brother. It's you ignorant-ass fools who believe being smart has something to do with the white man. Now, let's go. Like right now."

Jeebie might be the Lord but evidently Mr. Hakim was God, 'cause Jeebie slithered on back over to his car and got in it. Then he just drove off.

I breathed again and tried to tell myself all this shaking I was doing wasn't gon' help. But I couldn't stop until the minibus, with the words SAVE THE CHILDREN AT-RISK FOUNDATION on its side, rolled up. I read the words again. I wasn't getting in no van that had no shit like that on it. So I said, "May I have the address? I'd rather take the city bus over to your place."

I knew this was gon' get hard because the blond girl driving got out of the minibus and walked around to me and said, "I'm sorry. But you have to follow the rules. I hope you understand. We have gone to a lot of trouble to make sure we're here to pick you up on time."

I didn't move for fear I was turning into a violent person just like they said about black people, 'cause smacking her was what was going through my head.

"Okay," she continued, "so let's begin on a cooperative note. How about—you can choose any seat you want in the minibus? See?" She pointed inside. There were two kids I didn't know already watching me through the window. Actually one, 'cause the other one had her head down.

I wasn't going to start no war, so I just got in the van and took a seat across from the girl studying the stripes in her shorts. Then Ms. Responsibility turned to me as she strapped herself into the driver's seat "Oh, I'm Clarissa Montgomery. My father is a lawyer in town, and I'm a senior in high school. This is going to be fun. You'll see."

I still wanted to slap her, so I sat on my hands. I closed my eyes. If I was going to go to Fountainhead instead of Avery, I wasn't even gonna be looking.

A few stops later Betty, Kente, and Malik got on the minibus. Clarissa gave a welcome speech as they climbed inside.

I noticed only Malik mouthed thanks to her.

It made my cheeks burn that he'd said anything. When he passed by me he nodded but was silent.

Betty sat down beside me. Kente and Malik went to the last seats in the back.

"What's up?" Betty said.

"Nothin'," I said, rolling my eyes.

"You got that right," she said.

I looked at her and smiled.

She pointed out the window and said in a high-pitched proper voice, "Oh my God, this neighborhood is gonna kill us."

We both burst out laughing.

"That's a tough bracelet you got there," I said. "You make it?"

"Yeah. I made it. It's the colors of the Ethiopian flag. Red, gold, yellow, and green. My cousin is a Rasta. He's got locks, you know some people call them dreads, and everything. He even met Bob Marley."

She held out her arm for me to look closer.

"Ain't this a trip," she continued loudly. "I don't feel like getting up early in the morning and going nowhere in the summer. Shit. I usually sleep in the summer."

"I'm sorry, but you can't use profanity on the bus," Clarissa said, eyeing us in the rearview mirror.

"That ain't so," Betty said. "I just did."

Everyone laughed except Clarissa.

And Malik.

I don't think he laughed, 'cause I turned around to see if he was laughing at her, too. But he was busy looking stern-faced and thumbing through a magazine.

"Your brother is weird," I said to Betty.

"Tell me about it," she said, grinning.

At the center we were all herded into a big gym. They asked us to take a seat on the floor. *The floor.* The counselors were all sitting in chairs up front along with Mr. Pierce and the woman who had been smacked with the blood at school that day. She said her name was Miss Troutman. She was a lawyer who had worked for the juvenile justice system for six years. But she gave it up to be the administrator of this program.

She really cared that we understood where she was coming from. So she was going to use words we could understand easily. If there were any words we didn't recognize, all we had to do was raise our hands and she would provide us the definition. She continued smiling at us as she talked: "I saw the great need to intervene in the lives of criminals early, so that's why my partner and I in the law firm quit our positions and started this nonprofit program. Now we make only minimum salaries, but we love it. And we feel strongly we're doing something to make the world a safer place for all of us."

I was sitting on my hands again, not 'cause I wanted to slap her but because I was tempted to raise my hand for each word she used and wait for the definition. I knew that would be stupid, but so was her telling us that we didn't have sense enough to understand plain English.

I didn't think the other kids cared what she was talking about in any language, 'cause they either were drawing on their pads, whispering or checking each other out.

Malik was asleep, actually lying down on the floor. His hands folded over the magazine on his chest. His eyes closed, snoring.

I tried to read the magazine headline upside down but I couldn't make out anything but the word "figures." It must be about models or something. Maybe a Victoria's Secret catalog.

Miss Troutman explained she was passing the ball over to Mr. Pierce. He began, "You all know by now I'm Mr. Pierce. We're going to use sports metaphors to help you grasp what we're saying. We don't plan to diss your world."

He stopped as though he had been interrupted by applause. When nobody even coughed or looked up at him, he continued.

"This summer we're going to expose you, oops," he said, "I mean we're going to shoot the ball in brand-new nets. I'm not going to actually be around because I'm more the fund-raiser. But I assure you, everyone is going to have a good time. We'll take you to the symphony, the museum, the planetarium . . . how many of you know what that is?"

Betty raised her hand.

"Okay, Betty isn't it? What do you think the planetarium is?" He had a smirk on his face.

Betty cleared her throat. "Something to do with a plant."

Some of the counselors smiled; one black girl counselor snickered.

I cut my eyes at her to let her know I had her number. I turned back quickly.

Miss Troutman shook her head, no.

Mr. Pierce said, "Anybody else?"

I wanted to say it was a machine that let you see a make-believe sky with stars and planets. Plus, I didn't think Betty's answer was so bad. I could see why a person could assume the word had to do with plants. But I didn't say anything. Instead, I stayed sitting on my hands and wished I was somewhere else—specifically Avery.

This gym thing went on far too long. Each counselor had a little "I'm here to help" speech, and then it was time for lunch. We ate. Some of the kids said grace before they ate. Me, I didn't. My grandma said God has already blessed the food. How else would we have it?

Betty sat with me. She traded me her bologna sandwich for my tuna.

"That was dope," she said. "You know, what you did to Ms. Hill the other day. I can't stand her ass."

"Me either," I said.

"Why was you mad at her, though?" Betty said, passing her cake to me. "You want this? I gotta watch my weight."

"Sure, I'll take it. It's a long story."

"What? Tell me. I promise I won't tell nobody. First, I thought you was saying something about a school. But then I thought, ain't nobody getting *mad* over *not* going to school, you know what I'm saying."

"I was supposed to go to Avery University this summer. I plan to be a doctor."

"Damn. A doctor, huh. You must be smart. That's why you take that tenth-grade class?"

"I suppose," I said, not wanting her to think I had the big head.

"My brother is smart."

"Who?" I said.

"Who? Malik, stupid. You *know* Kente ain't smart."

I wanted to say I doubted Malik was smart, since I knew he'd been held back last year. But I didn't have to say it. She obviously figured my frown was for something.

"I know. He got left back. But it wasn't his fault. My mama and daddy were sick, and he worked to help us out."

"Oh. That's too bad," I said. "Are your mama and daddy better?"

She shrugged. "That hen's calling us again," she said, pointing to Clarissa.

Clarissa settled everybody back on the gym floor.

Then Miss Troutman went up front. She said, since it was the first day, we would get out early. And we did.

They trippin'. Why didn't she just say that without making us all sit back on the floor again? We rode back home on that same ugly minibus. When we got to the Shabazzes' stop I could see a man slumped out on their stoop.

"What up," Betty said. "You want some company?"

I didn't know what to say. Mama was cool about company, we just didn't have a lot of it. "Sure. You can hang out with me and Rhenda," I said, wondering why she wanted to go home with *me?*

When Kente walked up to her he said, "What you gon' do?"

Betty tilted her head sideways toward me. "I'm going with her home."

"Yeah. I'm going to shoot ball, then. See you later, aw-right."

Malik was standing behind him, reading his magazine. "Hey," he said, leaning over to Betty. "Stay late, okay. I'll take care of it by the time you come home." Then he touched her lightly on the shoulder and started off the minibus. But when he got up to the front, Clarissa stopped him.

She was talking low, and I had to strain to hear her.

She said, "I know that magazine. Which pictures are you checking out?"

I thought to myself, how does that heifer know he's not reading the damn thing? Then my heart stopped beating. Malik Shabazz, who rarely talked and never smiled, was up there grinning. I had never seen Malik grin before.

That girl makes me sick.

Betty didn't talk much after we got to my house. And when she did, she was talking softer—most times she talked loud, like she was in a shouting match and she was gonna win.

I walked her in the kitchen and introduced her to Rhenda, who was cooking spaghetti sauce while holding Tomika on her hip.

"Why are you cooking so early?" I asked her. "Mama ain't getting up until later. And I told you we were eating at that program."

"Sauce gotta simmer, that's why. It would be better if

we didn't eat it until tomorrow, but ain't nothing else here for me to cook."

I just shook my head in wonder. Rhenda watched too many cooking shows. I don't see why she can't just buy that jar sauce and be done with it. But no, she's got to chop up everything and take forever to cook it.

Mama was 'sleep in her room. It was after two o'clock. I knew she'd be getting up to eat later. We eat supper with Mama most nights.

Rhenda called me back in the kitchen the minute me and Betty sat down in the living room. "Hey, you tell Mama you was bringing that girl home?"

"Rhenda, why don't you put Tomika *down*," I said. "She ain't gonna *never* walk if you keep holding her."

"You dippin' in the ice cream and don't know the flavor. Now answer my question."

"Oh, so you can dip, huh. But I can't."

"If y'all want to eat. Yep."

I shook my head. "You trippin', girl. No. She just asked me if she could come. She's not even talking to me, really. I think she came to get away from a man I saw sitting on her stoop. Maybe, I don't know. Why? You think Mama is gon' be upset?"

"No," Rhenda said, smiling. "I'm the one upset. It means I have to cook more sauce."

I rolled my eyes. "Get real. How much sauce you think she gon' eat?" I said, walking back into the living room.

"You want to hear some music?" I asked Betty.

"Sure. What you got?"

"You know. Usher, Tyree, and Ginuwine. My brother Punky got Snoop, Puffy, and his crew. What you want to hear?"

She shrugged. "I'm down wid' that."

I put on Usher.

Mama came out rubbing her eyes just as the song started.

"Hey, Mama," I said quickly. "This is my friend Betty." Sometimes Mama say silly stuff when she first wake up. Best she know we got company.

"Oh, hi Betty," Mama said. "Good to meet you. I see y'all don't care nothing 'bout waking your mama up. I guess I'm going to have to sit in here with you then. Rhenda," Mama yelled toward the kitchen, "go *lay* that baby down. I saw her when I came in here. She's 'sleep, lying on your shoulder. You crazy girl, you can't cook with that baby slung on your hip like a sack of potatoes." Then Mama turned back to us.

"What's your last name Betty?"

"Shabazz."

"Oh, Lord. You named after Dr. Betty Shabazz. Your mama is right on time, honey. God. You 'bout what, fifteen? Your mama was definitely with it, wasn't she, girl? People barely knew who Betty Shabazz was when you was born. They barely knew who Malcolm was till the white man got ready for them to know. Of course, like the Muslims say, Always ready to give us a dead leader."

"Mama, please," I said, not wanting her to get on her pulpit.

"You got a nice place," Betty said.

"Thanks," Mama replied. "It's okay."

I didn't know what to make of that. Our place was okay—but *nice?* "Betty is going to that program with me, Mama."

"Yeah. Is that right? Did y'all have a good time today?" Mama asked. "Keisha, did you tell them you ain't gone be there long?"

Betty looked at me. "Where're you going?"

"I told you, Avery," I said.

"Oh," she said, looking down at her hands, picking at her cuticles.

Mama said, "I hope you're staying for dinner, Betty."

"I would like to, if it's okay."

"Sure it is. Do you live far?"

"No, over on Beaker."

"I see," Mama said, shaking her head. "I used to know some folks over on Beaker. Probably not your folks, though. Well, you're welcome over anytime. Keisha needs a good girlfriend, don't you, Keisha?"

I shook my head yes, even though Rhenda was always the only girlfriend I ever needed. But Mama was right. Rhenda was growing older now and since she's had Tomika, she didn't hang like she used to.

"Come over here, Keisha," Mama said.

I got up and walked to her.

"Ain't you forgot something?" Mama said, smiling up at me.

I didn't want to but I smiled like an automatic door opener.

"I think you got something belong to me, girl."

"Nope. I don't think so."

Then she pulled me down on her lap. "You got my hugs and kisses," Mama said as she hugged and kissed me on the forehead and cheeks. "These younguns," she said, looking at Betty, "always stealing my hugs and kisses."

"Mama!" I protested. "You're embarrassing me. I'm too big for this silly game," I whined, knowing full well we did this all the time.

"Silly game? Uh-huh. You showing out for Betty, huh? That girl comes crawling on my bed every afternoon hugging up under her mama. Don't let her fool you. And besides, I'll hug whoever I want in this house. This *my* house."

I sighed. There was no use.

"I'll be back," Mama said, letting me go and getting up from the chair. "I'm going out to call Punky. That boy. I'm gon' whip him good if he don't stay 'round closer to here. He thinks he's grown. All y'all too grown."

When Mama came back she made Punky set the table for not being home when she got up. He slammed down stuff so hard, Mama had to warn him twice. But by the time we ate he was back to hisself.

He knew he'd better be, if he didn't want his butt whipped. Mama didn't play.

Betty made a hit with Rhenda 'cause she kept complimenting her cooking. "That girl can burn," she said about a million times.

And 'bout a billion times Punky said, "She sure can burn," and then he'd fall out laughing.

"Okay. Okay," I finally said. "It was funny the first time, Punky, but that's enough."

Then he started beating on the table with a spoon and making raps out of every sentence anybody said.

I was glad when we were finished and could get out of the kitchen.

Rhenda said she'd wash the dishes.

Mama went back to bed.

And me and Betty went outside on the stoop.

"What time you got to go home?" I asked her. It was getting dark.

"It don't matter when I go," she said.

"What do you mean? Your mama at work or something?"

"You could say that. Hey, your sister is all right. I wish I had a sister, you know what I'm saying."

"Yep. I love having Rhenda most of the time. Unless she starts bugging and getting on my nerves. She's much nicer since Tomika been born, though."

"That's a pretty little baby. She's quiet, too. Don't do no whole lot of crying. I wanted to hold her. I love holding babies. I'm gonna have a baby one day all to myself. She gonna love her mama too."

"Yeah. She's a sweet baby," I said, thinking Betty say that now 'cause she ain't got no clue what Rhenda go through keeping that baby. Then I started wondering when Mama was going to come out and say something about Betty still being on the stoop.

"You got a best friend?" Betty asked me.

"No. Well, yeah, Rhenda."

"Oh," Betty said, picking at her fingernails.

I could hear it now. Something sad in her voice. She started twirling her long hair around her finger. She had light-colored brown hair, sort of gray-green cat eyes, and skin 'bout the color of cinnamon toast. She didn't look like Malik or Kente. They both were about my color. Malik had naturally curly hair and dark eyes. He and Betty had the same skinny nose but they still didn't look alike. I knew they were all half sister and brothers, but I wondered how that could be since Malik was older than her, and Kente younger. Maybe her mama adopted her?

"I like your mama, too," she said, still twisting her hair. "She's dope."

"Yeah. She's okay unless she's pissed off about something. Then all she knows is punishing somebody. She always says the same thing over and over, she can be sho'nuf scratching. Smart girls don't make dumb mistakes. Rhenda says that's Mama's rap."

Mama came to the door that minute. "I hear you out here," she said, laughing. "I got supersonic ears, remember. And you, Betty, how you getting home? Somebody coming to pick you up?"

"Yeah," Betty said. "I got to meet them at the corner store at eight o'clock."

"Them who?" Mama said, frowning.

"My two big brothers," Betty said with a straight face.

"The next time you tell them to walk here and meet you. That store ain't no place for no girl standing 'round. Ain't nothing but drug dealers and winos up there."

"Sure will," Betty said, staring at me.

I knew it wasn't true. At least I thought it wasn't true. Did her brothers know where I lived? They could, maybe. I was pretty sure they didn't say they were meeting her when they got off the minibus. But maybe they had a code. They seem to know she wasn't getting off with them when we pulled up to their stop. Hey, it's all that. Me, Rhenda, and Punky have codes between each other. Who was I to say she was lying? I just kept my mouth shut.

When Mama closed the screen door, I said, "Your brothers know where I live?" and she completely ignored my question.

"You want to be my best friend?" she asked me.

She was looking so serious. I shook yes. I did. There was something about her that I liked. She talked tough, but I could tell she was mostly talk. I'd seen that in school even though I didn't know her good. I knew that she'd taken up for some girl that people was picking on in gym.

"Cool," she said, smiling. "Here," she said, handing me the friendship bracelet she'd made.

"I can't take your bracelet," I said.

"You got that right," she said. "You can't. I gave it to you, shorty." She stood up. "See you tomorrow."

"It's not eight o'clock yet," I said, wishing she'd stay longer. It was kind of fun to have someone besides Mama, Rhenda, and Punky to talk to. I wasn't exactly the most popular girl at school. It was hard being friends when I had to study all the time.

"I gotta go," she said. "Later."

And just like that, she walked up the street, alone. I

fingered the bracelet and watched her disappear into the night. I have a best friend, I thought to myself. Betty Shabazz is one of my best friends. Then I laughed. Dummy—other than Rhenda, she your only friend.

I loved the planetarium best of the places we visited the first week 'cause it was the one thing that proved we are all the same. Everybody can see the night sky. Except maybe prisoners. When it comes to the night sky, we all equal, we all get a chance to see the Big Dipper and stuff. See, the sky ain't like the ocean or the mountains. I been reading a lot of books that let me know sooner or later, in order to live next to the ocean or high up in the mountains, you gonna have to have money. Maybe it ain't like that everywhere yet, but it's coming. I can tell.

But not the sky. Rich folk can't do shit about who is

seeing the sky. Even if they tried, I believe God would find a way to help us. You know, maybe a bad storm just comes one night and rips the roof off. The night sky is like all our dreams and hopes piled up where can't nobody reach 'em to tear 'em down. As long as there's stars in the sky, we gonna be all right. My grandma taught me that before she died—and I believe *her*. My grandma say, "Some people think that being poor is the same thing as being a criminal. Rich folk act like ain't nothing but poor folk got the devil in 'em, but honey, just 'cause we poor don't mean we born in sin."

My grandma, she won't never one of those church-goers, but she believed in God. My mama, now, she go to church and take us with her sometime. When we was little it was all the time. I don't go to church always, but I believe in God. And I still have hope. That's why I'm not giving up on Avery. Ms. Oliver will help me.

When I got home after the planetarium visit, Mama waved an envelope at me as I came in the door. "You got some mail, girl."

I ripped the sides and opened the letter. I was grinning from one ear to the other. I got all A's except conduct. But who cares? I showed the report card to Mama and Rhenda. Then we was all grinning.

"I'm applying to Avery, Mama," I said. "It's too late now, but first thing in the morning before I go to the center, I'm calling."

"Can you do that?" Mama asked me.

"She ought to do it," Rhenda said. "Why couldn't she?

She still got that Ms. Oliver to stick up for her. Ain't you?"

"Yep," I said, "And I could just leave the center and go. I mean, I've already filled out the preliminary papers with Ms. Oliver."

"Go for it, then," Mama said. "You want me to call for you?"

I didn't. I wanted to do it myself. All on my own. My grades were great and I couldn't see anything that could stop me. I found the copy of the preapplication I had filled out and called the next morning before I left for the center.

The woman on the phone was very nice and assured me I could send my mother's permission letter in right away. I had to have a personal interview before everything was final. She'd send me out the information about that. Then she made me an appointment for the following month. She said I could do the last six-week session, to make up the orientation sessions I'd missed this summer. The woman took my name, address, and the number from the form I'd filled out.

"Everything is all set."

"I thought maybe I could do the late summer program?" I said, feeling like I couldn't swallow my own spit.

"Sorry," the woman said. "That's filled up already. But it won't be a problem to add you to the fall program. Schools often let kids go half days when they have other projects like ours."

I felt the tears welling up in my eyes. I glanced over at Mama.

She had come home early, sitting right by the phone,

looking dead in my mouth. When I hung up she didn't say anything.

"They said I couldn't do the summer one. But I could do fall. September fifteenth to October thirtieth, and then officially start the program."

"That's good, though, baby. Ain't nothing wrong with that," Mama said, smiling. "You can finish this center thing. You said yourself you liked going on the trips."

I could tell she was putting up a good front. Trying to make me feel okay about it. But I didn't feel okay, really. I was disappointed. What if I couldn't do the September thing? What if the guidance counselors wouldn't let me out of school early? There were so many if's. It wasn't fair. But what else could I do? At least there was a way to make up for the missed sessions. I shrugged. "You're right, Mama. I'm cool. I can hang out at the center."

That morning when I went to the program I felt happier than I'd felt since the day Ms. Hill called me in that room. I was going to attend Avery after all. I smiled. Me at Avery. Me a doctor. A real doctor helping people out. Making sure ain't no more preemie babies born. Yeah. That's me, Dr. Keisha Wright.

The second week at the center we went swimming. We rode in three vans to get there, all of the counselors announcing on the way to everybody we met that we the at-risk kids. It was all right since we was now calling the program BARF among ourselves.

There were two black counselors: one named Phyllis,

who I didn't think about, and one I didn't like much who called herself "Kimmie." Her name was Kimberly Wellsley. She was the one who'd snickered at Betty when she'd offered her planetarium definition. I'd been right—Kimmie was one of those people you needed to always walk *behind*. And, if somehow she ended up behind *you*, your job was to remove all sharp objects from her hands first, 'cause she'd stab you in a minute, if you know what I'm saying.

I heard her telling some of the white girls that black girls who live in the ghetto can't play soccer or tennis but they know how to play basketball just like a boy. She actually squealed that she was teaching herself the game so she could coach us.

The only white people on the vans were three of the counselors, plus Miss Troutman and two very tall white boys who just got out of a special private school. That's juvenile detention to anybody who don't know.

We went all the way to the coast of Georgia to a beach—a real beach with ocean water going out as far as you can see. They had lifeguards. And believe me they needed 'em 'cause most poor people I know in the inner city don't have nowhere to be learning to swim. That is unless they live near the Martin Luther King Jr. Aquatic Center. But don't nobody I know go there.

None of us had been to a beach before. I wanted to stand there and watch the waves curling up onto the white sand forever. I wanted to build a tent at the water's edge and sleep there at night, listening to the sound of God's breathing and watching God's television in the sky.

But the counselors started giving orders and broke my spell.

So at first we were scared of the water. Clarissa was with me and Betty. She was saying to us, "Come on, now," like we babies who were being silly being afraid of the dark. But anybody with sense knows there can things in the dark to fear.

"I'm going to be with you," she said. "There is nothing to be afraid of. I'll be here to help you."

I touched my toe in the water. It was cold, way colder than it looked. With the sun shining it looked like it ought to be warm. Like when you stepped down in it you were gon' feel like you in a big old bubble bath. But it didn't feel that way. Goose bumps popped up all over my body. I didn't have on a swimming cap and I didn't want my hair to get wet. I had a brand-new navy blue swimming suit with silver stars on it 'cause my mama knows I love me some stars. My mama bought the swimsuit just for this.

Betty had on black shorts and a white T-shirt.

"You scared?" I asked her. "I ain't never been in no water for swimming before."

"I been once. With Malik. He can swim. They taught him in the Boys Club."

"Oh," I said, looking over at him.

He was standing a ways up the beach. I could see he had a muscled-looking chest. I looked up to his face and he was staring in my direction. Different. Sort of like he was hungry. And for some reason that look made me feel warm and tingly inside.

Clarissa yelled, "Come on, follow me!" She was facing us, walking backwards into the water.

Betty was directly in front of her and she was following her like a sheep.

I stepped one foot into the water and then two, then I took a step, another step, another, and so on until we were far out. Much farther than I wanted to be.

Betty strutted out into the water even farther than Clarissa. She lifted her leg up and took a giant step. "See," she called back. "This is easy."

Clarissa shouted, "Betty you're out too far. Come on back now."

Suddenly Betty disappeared. All you could see was her arm stretched up out of the water.

I waited for her to jump back into view and say something smart.

She didn't, and I realized Clarissa was running in the water toward her.

Clarissa stumbled, then grabbed her foot.

She must have stepped on something. She'd warned us on the bus about jellyfish.

Clarissa was sort of hopping quickly now through the water toward Betty.

But Betty was even farther out. Moving on top of a wave. I saw Betty's head pop up. She scrambled for a second, throwing up her arms, and then her head swooped under the water again. Her arms were splashing water all around. Another huge, soapy-looking wave grabbed her up and threw her like she was a ball bouncing on the pavement.

I heard myself scream. The wind had picked up since we'd arrived, and the waves were getting bigger. Out over the water the clouds were that I'm-gonna-get-you gray. Grandma would see those kind of clouds, and say, "God's pissed off again 'bout something."

Clarissa called frantically to the lifeguard: "A girl—drowning—over here—hurry."

I looked up toward where the lifeguard sat. He wasn't that far away. He was looking through binoculars in Betty's direction, a tall, blond, Fabio-looking guy standing high on a platform.

I knew he must have seen Betty flapping around and slurping up water, her head bopping in and out between tiny yelps.

He set the binoculars down. Unbuttoned his shirt and folded it. Pulled off his flip-flops. Shook his left leg and then his right leg.

"Hurry up!" Clarissa shouted to him. "She's being dragged into deep water."

Clarissa was struggling against the waves toward Betty.

Another huge one lifted Betty into the air like she was on a carnival ride. It slammed her away. She bobbed up, went under, moved farther out. Bobbed under, then up.

"Help! Somebody help!" Clarissa screamed.

She was hysterical now. I didn't know if anyone could hear her screaming out there. I couldn't even see Betty anymore, just huge rolls of foam. I cupped my hand over my eyes and searched the water for the lifeguard. I saw him. He was strolling out into the water, in no hurry. He moved like a man walking an old tired dog, not somebody trying to help save a drowning girl.

I saw a spot of red. I was scared 'cause I could only think of one thing that made red and that was blood. But then I saw black. Black skin glistening in the water. Was it Betty? I thought she had on a white T-shirt and black shorts? No, not Betty. Clarissa? I could see Clarissa treading in the water, moving her arms around frantically and sort of bobbing out of sight when the waves hit her body.

And then I saw it was Malik in red swimming trunks. He was carrying his sister out of the water in his arms, holding her up like she was some kind of offering to God, looking like a knight in shining armor. A black knight. He waded onto the sand, walked up the beach a ways, and laid his sister down.

Betty was quickly swallowed up in a circle of counselors, and then another lifeguard showed up that I hadn't seen.

The lifeguard in the water was strolling back toward the beach, his muscled body shimmery with drops of water, his long, stringy blond hair clinging 'round his face and shoulders.

And then I saw the red streaking again out into the water. It was Malik. He grabbed the lifeguard by the head and shoved him under a wave. They were fighting. I could tell that now. The lifeguard might have muscles, but Malik was almost as big and he had another weapon more powerful than any muscles—fury.

I saw two other white lifeguards racing toward the water.

Kente saw them, too, and he yelled, "I'll kill y'all if you hurt my brother," and took off after them.

Then the two delinquent white boys ripped off their T-shirts and headed for Malik and the lifeguard, too.

I yelled to the remaining three black boys standing on the beach watching. "Get your butts in there and help Malik." I didn't want this to be a race thing; but this is what it's always about, ain't it?

Two of the black boys ran toward the water. The other one said, "Hell, I don't give a shit about Malik. I got to think about my own ass."

I walked over to him. I gritted my teeth and balled up my fist. I wanted to hit him so bad, my nose started bleeding. I pinched it, held my head back, and said, "You know what? You know what Chris Rock say, don't you? You one of them niggers he be talking about."

I ain't never called a black person a nigger in my life. Not even fooling around. My mama didn't play that, and I didn't like it. But now I knew who Chris Rock was meaning.

This fool was so stuck on hisself, he didn't see that if he'd been the one out there drowning, that white boy wouldn't have saved him, either. And I'd bet money Malik would'a still cared enough about him to jump that guard on his account.

As my mama said, some people don't know nothing 'bout themselves. When you black, you never escaping that fact, so you gon' have to do the best you can with it. You can't let nobody stop you from believing in yo'self. And always protect your own.

I waded out into the shallow water. I was scared, but I wanted to see what was happening. Malik was whupping all three of them white boys, with the help of Kente, the other two black boys, and to my surprise the two delinquent white boys. Maybe it ain't about being black after all: maybe it's like my grandma say, it's about sticking together when ain't none of you got nothing.

I heard a siren in the background and I turned to see not an ambulance but the police. The cops, all white, jumped out of their car, batons ready, holding their guns at their sides as they ran. They whipped off their shoes and socks, waded into the water knee-deep, and one of them yelled, "Stop now or we'll shoot every last one of you."

I suspected they didn't mean the white boys, but I couldn't know for sure since some cops, black or white, don't mind shooting whenever they have an opportunity.

The commotion in the water stopped slowly. Malik was bleeding, but so was everyone else. The white boys were the most bloody and bruised.

I couldn't see Malik's bruises. He ran out of the water and past the cops at a jog.

The cop in charge snatched a radio off his belt and shouted into it, "One of the black ones is on foot getting away. Get him."

There were at least six cop cars now.

Malik pushed into the circle of people surrounding Betty.

I raced out of the water and saw him on his knees, wiping his sister's hair back from her face.

"You aw-right?" he asked her over and over.

I could not move from my spot. Malik stroked Betty's forehead real gentle-like. I had never seen a man be so gentle and look so concerned over a girl. Punky would be that way if something happened to me. But Punky didn't have that body. And Malik was not my brother.

I watched each muscle rippling in and out as he stroked Betty. His back looked strong, like he could pick up a house on it. Malik was strange to me. And I felt funny inside watching him.

The cops pushed through and snatched up Malik.

"Let him alone!" I yelled as they gathered us up and herded us to the vans. I don't know why, but I felt like I should be the one who defended him. I wasn't the only one looking at him though. All the girls chattered like a bunch of chickens about what Malik had done.

After the cops had loaded us all back on the vans, they stood listening to the counselors and Miss Troutman trying to convince them not to arrest Malik.

Three cops were listening to the lifeguard's story. He was talking loud, and I could hear each word like a knife. I stuck my head out the van window and shouted, "He's lying like a dog. He wasn't even trying to save Betty."

The cop in charge walked away from Malik, back toward our van. He said to the lifeguard, "The boy says you were taking your time. Not acting like the girl might be drowning."

The lifeguard said, "You know how these people lie. God. I had to put my stuff down, then strip, and I was there. She was too far out and she had on black and she was black and shit. I couldn't make her out in the water. Damn. You'd think I did something wrong."

The cop shouted to the men surrounding Malik. "Let the boy go. Bring him up here and put him on the van." Then he looked directly at the lifeguard. "You're lucky this time. You better think about getting another job."

I smiled and sank back in the seat. My grandma told me not all white people mean and crazy—and maybe she was right, maybe they ain't.

Malik's eye and hand were swollen really big. He sat in the back of the bus on a seat alone, his head in his lap.

Betty sat leaning against Kente shivering and still crying.

I felt bad for all three of them. For all of us. The only thing these white folks was going to remember was that we was fighting. Ain't no doubt in my mind they gon' forget why.

There was only one lesson I was taking back with me from this trip. I thought about it as I heard Miss Troutman's lecturing behind talking about what we'd learned today. My one lesson was, I was going to learn how to swim. 'Cause the next black person I saw drowning, I wanted to be able to save 'em myself.

I persuaded Miss Troutman that it would be a good idea to offer swimming lessons for anyone who was interested. She decided we should attend the Martin Luther King Jr. Aquatic Center at least for a few weeks. Both Clarissa and Kimmie had to take us since there were so many of us.

The number of supervisors on outings was one of Miss Troutman's "great things about this program." Four girls, plus me, and six boys signed up. I was surprised to find out Betty was one of the four.

The swimming pool was nothing I could have imagined. I'd never been in a chlorine-enclosed place before. The smell stopped my breathing from coming easy. It ain't like Clorox—it's mustier than that. The water is bluish-green, looking like the ocean looks on television. Sort of a minty mouthwash look. And the noise is like the freeway.

We undressed and changed into our swimsuits. Kimmie didn't get in the water. She let her feet dangle over the edge while she read her fashion magazine. She said she'd prefer to watch from the sidelines. She meant watch her magazine, I guess.

Clarissa jumped into the pool first. The other kids walked down the steps into the water. But I was too dog-gone nervous to set my foot on the cement steps. They looked like they were swaying beneath the water.

I watched Clarissa wade out till the water came up to her chest. "See, this isn't like the ocean. Until you get to that rope over there, the water doesn't get much deeper. Come on, Keisha. This was your idea, wasn't it?"

There were a lot of people splashing and swimming in this pool. Shouts, whistles, and loud laughing bounced off the walls all around us.

I suspected by Clarissa's tone she was going to try to find ways to punish me. Not because she didn't love to swim, but I'd bet a Coke it was because all the people in this pool were black. I don't mean it was segregated.

That's illegal. But what I mean is, it's a pool where few white people ever come. See, that's how integration really works. They ain't stopping you, they just ain't gon' be where you at.

Betty waded out into the water with Clarissa. I watched her and thought, Wow. Ain't no way. A week ago she almost drowned!

A man came up beside me and said, "What's the problem? You scared to get in the water?"

I shook my head yes. My body was trembling all over because they'd made me shower and not dry off and it was getting cold standing in the air.

"I tell you what," he said. "What if I go in the water and then hold your hand while you step in. How about that?"

He said it in a way I could know he meant it. Immediately I felt some level of trust for him, something in his eyes.

"I'm Mr. Walt," he said.

I felt like he wasn't gon' let me drown or let my head go under the water, unless he went under, too, and drowned with me. So I shook my head okay.

I saw a little frown of hurt pass over Clarissa's face. Maybe she didn't want to be here, but I could see she wasn't used to not being trusted, either. People trust white people until they do something wrong. They trust black people when they prove they gon' do something right.

Clarissa said, "Go ahead. Let him help you." She waded over to talk to the "Kimmie girl." That's what I called her because she was so fake. I was positive that, like Clarissa, she didn't want to be here, or around any black people. It didn't matter that she was black as coal.

Mr. Walt held his hand out and grasped my wrist gently. "Come on. I promise I won't turn you lose until you're ready."

I stepped down in the water and smiled. I thought of when I was twelve years old and I joined my mama's church. One Sunday I got baptized. That's likely the first time you gotta trust somebody with keeping you safe, other than your own family.

The thought came clear to me that day as I listened to the choir sing, "Take me to the water. Take me to the water. Take me to the *wat . . . er*. To be baptized." I could hear the guitar, the piano, and the drums playing, all just for me. I could feel all the people there, watching for me to be in that water. I was scared that day, too.

I had on an ankle-length white dress with a white towel wrapped around my head, flowing down my back like it was long hair. Miss Beulah had on her white choir robe, with a white towel slung across her shoulder. She was holding me by the waist, whispering, "Don't be scared now, baby. You gon' be fine. The Lord don' called you and you ready to come. The water ain't gon' hurt you none."

I asked for the millionth time, "Is Reverend Covington gon' hold my head under the water long? Suppose they drop me? Suppose I drown?"

"First off," she said, "would Reverend Covington or Brother Johnnie let you drown?"

I shook my head no.

"See. They gon' dip you in there so fast, you won't even know you wet. You'll see."

The pool was in front of the wall that's behind the pulpit. If it ain't time for someone to be baptized, you don't even know it's there. They have these red velvet drapes that can close up so you can't see the pool in the floor back there.

I stepped down into the water. My white dress billowed out around me. I could hear Miss Beulah on the side of the pool whispering over and over again, "Thank you, Jesus. Yes, Lord. Thank you, Jesus."

The red velvet curtains were open. And you could see the picture of a brown-skinned Jesus painted behind the pool on the wall. I was glad they took away the white-looking Jesus. This Jesus looked like me. Like he might actually care what was going to happen to me here. He was holding a white sheep in his arms. I loved that picture.

I looked up at Jesus to see if he was watching. He was smiling down at me, and I felt a little bit better.

Reverend Covington reached up and took my hand. And then Brother Johnnie took my other hand, and they led me to the center of the pool. Reverend Covington and Brother Johnnie both had on white robes. Miss Beulah had passed the towel to Reverend Covington, and it was now draped on his shoulder. "Keisha," he said, "this is a day to remember. No matter what you do in life you've given yourself to the Lord and there is always forgiveness and love with God."

"Yes, sir. But . . . but I'm . . . I'm scared."

"We all scared, Keisha. But being scared can't stop you, though. Remember, the Lord is always there. Now I'm going to place my hand on the small of your back, right here. And Brother Johnny is going to do the same. Then, just before we lean you back, I'm going to slip my other hand under your head so you won't have to worry about being under too long. Brother Johnnie's gonna pinch your nose so the water don't go in it. Okay? I'll give you a signal, and then you hold your breath and you'll be okay. You got any questions?"

I shook my head no, even though my mind was crammed with questions. But it didn't make no sense to ask them now.

I felt Reverend Covington's hand on my back. Then brother Johnnie's, and I felt safe. I could tell by the touch of their hands that I was safe from drowning. I could tell by the tremor in Reverend Covington's voice, rising and falling like the rhythm of the swing on my grandma's porch, that I was safe. And I could tell by their eyes that I was safe as I heard Reverend Covington say, "I baptize you in the name of the Father. In the name of the Son. And in the name of the Holy Ghost."

They dipped me under the water, and I believed I'd met God there. I don't even remember the signal. And when I came out I gasped for air, but I was still alive. To me this meant I was going to live my life in a good way. Try not to do nothing bad. And I was going to remember always that second of freedom, when my head lifted from the water, the drops, like rain, coming down on my face and the joy filling up my lungs. I knew then that you could stop breathing and still live. It was a new awakening for me. You could be scared and still do something you're afraid of. Being scared couldn't really stop you from doing what you wanted to do.

And now, feeling Mr. Walt's hand on the small of my back woke that feeling again. I stepped onto the bottom of the pool and felt the cement under my toes. It felt a little rougher than I'd expected. And in a minute Mr. Walt lead me out farther.

Betty yelled, "You go, girl." She was propped up on the other side of the pool with her elbows sort of holding her up, letting her legs float up in the water.

Mr. Walt told me to just do what he did, whenever I felt safe enough to do it. He bent his body over in the water and stretched out his arms and hands, palms under.

I watched him just leaning over there for a minute. I looked around to see if other people were laughing at me. But no one was watching. Not even Betty; she was drying off now. I stared back at Mr. Walt.

He didn't move his arms; he just let them bob up and down gently. His head wasn't in the water at all.

After watching him stand up and then stretch out again, I tried it.

Then, next, Mr. Walt just laid the top part of his face in the water while his arms were stretched out. He was taking a deep breath first, and then just laying his face in the water.

I thought, I can do that. A few minutes later I was doing it. We went on like this until I got to where I could bend my knees and let my full head sink under the water, my hair swelling out around me. I even forgot about all the noise.

Finally Clarissa, who'd been swimming on the other side of the rope, came over and said it was time to go. She said that Kimmie, Betty, and the others girls had already left to change. Clarissa got out of the pool and stood up on the side waiting for me.

When I stepped out I saw Malik up on the diving board—the tall one. I gasped and grabbed Clarissa's shoulder. I whispered to her, "They better tell him to get down before he falls." Swimming is one thing. Diving is another. I had never, ever seen a black person dive off a diving board.

Then Clarissa turned and saw Malik; she looked as alarmed as I felt. She called to Mr. Walt, who was on the other side of the pool putting on some gym pants.

"Sir," she called. "He's not supposed to be up on the diving board. Could you get him down before . . ."

Malik had left the platform. In the seconds we'd turned our eyes to Mr. Walt, Malik had disappeared. Did he climb down? Fall into the water? I looked around the sides of the pool. I didn't see him. I looked into the pool. There were only a few swimmers in the deep part, and no Malik.

Clarissa and I ran to the edge.

I knelt down beside her, scanning the water, and held my breath.

Mr. Walt jumped off into the deepest part of the pool, blowing a few shrills on his whistle. Three lifeguards in a split second dived in after him.

I looked out at the deep end, wondering why Malik's head didn't even come up and down, like drowners on TV. I wondered, just because you can swim doesn't mean you can dive, does it? Or was he trying to kill himself and just sink like a rock to the bottom and stay? I felt a tickle on my ankle. I reached down to brush off whatever was crawling on me—and screamed.

Malik's hand came up out of the water, barely brushing my leg. He grasped the edge of the pool and pulled himself up and out of the water. He came up almost between my legs, but I had already jumped back, still screaming.

"What? What?" he said, standing and shaking himself while whipping his head around, trying to figure the cause of my freaking out.

Clarissa jumped up off her knees. She was staring at him like he was one of the ghosts in *A Christmas Carol*.

Then she spoke: "Don't scare me like that, Malik. I thought you'd drowned." And then she hugged him.

I didn't move. I was in shock. *Clarissa hugged Malik.*

He quickly shoved her off him. "I'm cool," he said, and walked over to a bench and grabbed his towel. He wrapped it around his waist and disappeared into the doors of the locker room.

"Are you okay?" she asked me.

I didn't answer. I just stared at her.

"I didn't know he could dive," she said. "Did you? He is full of surprises, you know that?" she said, smiling and looking toward the locker room like she could see through the walls.

Kimmie walked over, fully dressed now. She frowned. "Like, what are you doing? Like, did you just like *hug* him?"

There was no question in my mind. Kimmie girl gave the word "like" a bad name.

Clarissa didn't answer her but looked at me. "Did you know he could dive?" she asked again.

I didn't answer her.

Kimmie interrupted, looking directly at me. "Kaleisha, hurry up. You're going to make us get back late."

I didn't correct her about my name or answer Clarissa. I just picked up my towel and walked to the dressing room downstairs. No, I didn't know Malik could dive. I mean, Betty told me he knew how to swim from the Boys Club, but I didn't know she meant swim like in really swim.

I didn't know what surprises Clarissa was talking about, either, unless it was about him grinning up in her face on the van that day. But what I did know was that she'd hugged him. She'd hugged Malik. But she hadn't hugged Betty when she almost drowned. It bothered me for some reason, but I didn't say nothing to Clarissa or Betty. I just got ready to go back to the stupid center.

I told Mama about my swimming and Mr. Walt. "He's the bomb. He's a swim coach, Mama. He says I can swim good. Me. Can you believe it? I swam across the pool."

"That's good," Mama said sleepily. "Now go on in there and clean up that house. It's dust everywhere in there. Can you swim that?"

A few days later at the center I was getting ready to leave for swim practice when I heard someone calling behind me. At first I didn't turn around.

"Excuse me. May I speak to you for a minute, Kaleisha?" Kimmie girl asked.

I stopped. What did *she* want? "My name is Keisha," I said.

"Sorry. Keisha. Would you, like, do me a favor? Since, I'm already doing you a favor by coming over to that pool."

"What?" I said, not wanting to be in a long conversation with someone who'd never even nodded at me.

"Well, like, my boyfriend, he's like a basketball star at William and Mary. And like, he's been away at school, and like, he'll be home soon, and I want to learn all I can about basketball so I can, like, surprise him. And he's like, always saying, I don't know anything about basketball. So, like, will you be on my basketball team that I'm starting?"

I was tempted to go, Like, well you know, like heck no. But I said, "If you don't know nothing about basketball how you gon' up and just start a team?" Clueless.

"See, well, it's like, I already asked Miss Troutman if I could be, like, the coach of the girls team. Like, I can learn better, like if I have like, hands-on experience. See, like I bought this really cool book that has like plays in it." She opened the book and stuck it out toward me.

I narrowed my eyes. "Are you for real?" I said, squinting like she might be, like, blinding me with that like bright high-and-mighty duh-ness.

"Like, I heard you could really play. So, like if you do it, like, I'll take you to meet Michael Jordan when he comes to town. My father like knows him personally. Please," she said, putting her hands up like she was praying.

67

I wanted to say, God should just smite you down right now. My grandma used to say that about people who just insult you to your face. If Grandma was around, I was sure this would be one of those times she'd approve. "I'm not interested," I said, and walked away. That girl works my last nerve. Does she not realize she's black? Like real black. I was glad to get out of there and ride the minibus to the pool. At least, I'd be away from her sorry behind since she always sat in the back reading her magazine.

By this time Mr. Walt had me gliding across the pool. Betty and the other girls had started taking a class with one of the other lifeguards. Clarissa had given me over to Mr. Walt and was now swimming with Malik. Sometimes I could hear them laughing together, and I'd forget what I was doing and gulp water. Nasty water. Even though the rule was you weren't supposed to pee in the pool, I for one, didn't believe everybody just automatically followed all the rules. And what about the snot and spit? I couldn't think about that or I'd never get in the water again. I pushed it all from my mind and concentrated on finding God in the water.

One week later I could swim. I don't mean glide, I mean do the backstroke, the butterfly, the sidestroke, freestyle, you name it I could do it. I could dive off the racing stands and I could swim the entire length of the pool, twenty-five yards. And fast, too. Real fast. Mr. Walt said I was a natural. He said after he saw me jump in the water head first, then from a sitting push off, then kneeling, then kneeling on one knee, then standing with cross-hands overhead, and then finally the one leg tip all in a few days, he knew.

He had quoted some statistics to us about swimming. He said according to a man named Jack Moore, a professor at the University of Southern Florida, once past age four, a black child was two to four times more likely to drown than a white child.

I thought, I'm not going to let that happen around me. So I swam.

"Hey, wait up." It was Malik. He was walking with his towel wrapped around his waist. The muscles in his chest bulging with each step.

"Yeah," I said, not sounding friendly. I was mad at him about something. Maybe that he was paying more attention to Clarissa than me. But at that time I didn't admit it, not even to myself.

"You want to learn how to dive?"

"Not from you," I snapped. And walked away.

I watched Malik climb up on the high diving board. Then he was in the water, a slight splash surrounding him as he disappeared—out of sight.

I found Mr. Walt. "I want to learn to dive off the high board."

"You sure you ready now?"

"Yep."

"Okay. I've been meaning to ask you, Keisha. How about joining our swim team here at MLK? We're getting ready for the Olympics. And to be honest, you swim better than anyone I've got. Technique and speed wise, plus you've got the perfect body shape and muscle tone.

Girl, you just a minnow waiting to be a shark. Ain't no doubt you were a fish in your last life, young lady. What do you say?"

Nobody had ever called me a young lady before. What was there left to say but "yes."

Then I remembered Mama. "What exactly will the team be doing?" Truth be told I didn't know much about the Olympics. I'd seen the ice-skaters before on TV, but that's about it.

Mr. Walt said that since the mid-80s, when Adolph Coors of the Coors Brewing Company made the statement that "blacks were unsuited for swimming because their nostrils were too big"—like we would inhale all the water—black coaches been pushing for black kids to get into swimming.

"We'll practice a lot," he said, "to prepare for competition."

"What's practice a lot?" I asked, frowning.

Mr. Walt smiled, "A lot is three or four times a week and sometimes more. To compete you're probably going to have to build up to at least ten to thirteen practices a week."

"What? What about my studies? I try to read a lot in the summers, Mr. Walt. I want to be a doctor. Not an athlete."

I was feeling a little like I'd just been smacked in the face by another Ms. Hill. Did he think all black kids ought to stick to rapping and playing sports?

"I want you to meet somebody tomorrow," he said. "Just think on joining the team for now."

"Who? Who do you want me to meet?"

"You'll see. It's a surprise. Who knows, Keisha, you might enjoy competing around here—then away—at other meets. Getting ready for the State Championships."

"When you say away, do you mean out of town?" I asked, realizing this was sounding more and more like, even if I wanted to, I wasn't going to be able to join.

"Yes. We'll ride the MLK van out of town. Sometimes, especially when school starts, we might even have to stay overnight. But we'll have chaperons."

"My mama," I said, clearing my throat, "doesn't allow any of us to spend the night anywhere, Mr. Walt. She thinks something might happen to us if she's not there—then she'd feel bad."

"She probably means spending the night with other kids. I can see that. But this is different. I don't think she'll mind."

Obviously he didn't know my mama. "She won't let me. I bet you. She's funny like that."

"Then what about I go talk to her?"

"I don't think that'll help. She says kids ain't got no business sleeping away from home, Mr. Walt. And I don't think just 'cause it's swimming, it'll make a difference."

"I tell you what, I'll take you home and we'll see? How about it?"

It never hurts to try, I thought. Plus, Mr. Walt was about my mama's age. Maybe he could reason with her. I had never figured her out when it came to spending the night away. She wouldn't even let me stay over with her own relatives.

Mr. Walt's car was nice. Not real fancy, but better than any car I'd ever been in. The seats were real leather and soft, too. I kind of hated it when we turned a corner into the project. Maybe for the first time I felt uncomfortable that we lived in public housing. I'm not sure why, but I felt funny. It could have been fear. I'd never even thought about getting nobody to talk to my mama before about something she already made a rule. She could go off. I hadn't considered that.

"Mr. Walt, maybe this isn't such a good idea," I said.

"You worried about what I'm going to say? Don't be. You'll see. I know what I'm doing, Keisha. Trust me."

I frowned. I had never been around a man long enough for him to even say those words to me, "Trust me." It sounded weird. Not right, coming from someone I really didn't know. Rhenda always said, when a man says, "Trust me," don't believe it. We pulled up in front of the house.

Now I was really unsure, but it was too late. Because the next thing I knew, I heard Rhenda screaming at me on my side of the car, "Look out."

Mama yanked Mr. Walt's driver's door open, shouting, "What in the hell are you doing with my daughter? Do you know she's not but fourteen years old. You old fart, I'm going to call the cops on you after I take care of you myself."

Mama was wielding her butcher knife dangerously close to Mr. Walt's head.

"Mama, Mama," I yelled. "This is Mr. Walt, the swimming coach I told you about."

Rhenda was already on the other side now, trying to

snatch the butcher knife away from Mama. Fool still had the baby on her hip.

"What are you doing?" I pleaded. "He just brought me home, that's all. Why you trippin' like this?"

I scrambled around to the other side, me and Rhenda trying to hold her back. "Mama," I cried, "he ain't mean no harm. I told him he could come talk to you. Why you doing this?"

I could feel her arm slacking some.

Mr. Walt had smartly closed his door and locked it.

Mama's fighting arm relaxed, and Rhenda took the knife.

"Why the hell didn't you call me and tell me he was bringing you home?" she said to me, tears streaming down her face. "You know you ain't allowed in no car unless I tell you."

"I'm sorry, Mama," I said. "Honest. I thought it would be okay since he's my coach. I told you about him, remember?"

"Yes, but I ain't say nothing to you about riding in no damn car with him, did I?"

"No, ma'am. I'm sorry." My mama hardly ever cursed. But when she did, you better believe she was mad. Mad and wild. It wasn't like she'd hurt us, but I felt sorry for anybody else who was around.

Mr. Walt rolled down the window, but not enough that she could stick her hand through it. "I'm sorry, Mrs. Wright. I should have called. It's not your daughter's fault. If I could just come in and speak with you, I can straighten this out."

My mama shrugged her shoulders and pulled away from me and Rhenda. "Come on in, then."

I could see she was sorry, and maybe a little embarrassed. Mama wasn't a violent person, so I couldn't figure out why she'd come bursting out of the house like that. But now she wasn't happy about what she'd done. I could tell.

Inside, she sat on the couch.

Mr. Walt took a chair near the door.

I figured that was smart. So in case he needed to get out fast, he could run.

"Mrs. Wright, listen," Mr. Walt began. "I apologize. It's just that I am so excited about your daughter's swimming and the possibility that she could be on the MLK swim team for the Olympics. She's the first girl I've ever had that I thought could make it. All the way. So it's my fault. I do know better than to ride a child in my car without the parent's permission. Again, I'm sorry. And I applaud you for coming after me like you did."

My mama looked up. "*I'm* sorry. I don't know what got into me. I actually know my own daughter better than that." Then she looked at me. "Keisha, I should know you wouldn't ride in a car unless you knew the person was safe. You're a good girl and you got common sense."

"It's okay, Mama," I said, but it really wasn't okay. I wondered why she had so many hang-ups about little things like that.

"Mama can go off sometimes for real," Rhenda said, and hugged Tomika, who was dozing, to her chest.

Mama said, "I'm gon' go off on you, Rhenda, if you don't go lay that baby down."

"Okay, I'll go lay down with her," Rhenda said. She knew that Mama didn't like her making a wise remark in front of company and her best bet was to disappear.

Mama looked at Mr. Walt. "Go on. It's always one thing or another. They can't just do it; it's got to be some words."

"Mrs. Wright," Mr. Walt continued, "I know you don't know me. But believe me, I have no bad intentions toward your daughter. I have a daughter Keisha's age. She lives with my ex-wife. And I wouldn't want an old man bringing her home, either. Believe me. I do understand your situation."

"What's your ex-wife's name?" Mama asked, leaning forward, staring at Mr. Walt now.

"Pearl Givens was her name before we married."

"Peaches?" Mama said hesitantly. "They used to call her Peaches, right?"

"Yes, you're on the right track."

"You used to be in a singing group? A gospel singing group in school?"

Now Mr. Walt was sitting up straighter himself, staring back. "I sure did."

"I thought you looked familiar when you came in the door. After I calmed down, I said to myself, I know *him*. Wow. Walter Bullock." Mama cleared her throat nervously. "It's been a long time. There's things back then I'd love to forget."

"It's okay. I forget lots of things lately. We all do. Some things *should* be forgotten."

"Yeah. You're right," Mama said, lifting her eyebrows. "Thanks," she said, sighing.

"Some things shouldn't, though," Mr. Walt said.

Mama sat up straighter. She acted as though she was holding her breath.

I sat up, too, now. Wondering was something going down that I'd missed. There was something weird about the way they were talking, but I couldn't be sure why I was feeling this way. They both looked funny to me. Like they had a secret together or something.

Finally Mr. Walt said, "Your mama was real smart in school."

"She was?" I asked. I guess I'd never thought of my mama as being smart in school. I knew she had good common sense and she was hardworking and stuff, but she ain't never talked much about her school days. What kind of secret was *that?*

"Yep. I remember you was like the top of the your class. In the ninth grade. Yeah, I remember that. People used to say you was the smartest girl ever come through our school. And the nicest girl too."

"Okay, enough about me," Mama said. "What is it you want with Keisha? Now that I know who you are, I think we can talk about it. After all, the one thing I remember about you was you was nice, a real gentleman. If I recall, you were always honest and forthright. You used to almost be like a junior preacher, always talking about religion in school."

"Yes. Got teased a lot for it. I'm a preacher now, in fact. And I still love the Lord better than anything in the world. That and my job coaching. I'm a swimming coach at Willow Bend High School. In the summer I coach at the Martin Luther King Jr. Aquatic Center, where your daughter has been swimming. And I can tell you in all my years I've never met any girl who can swim like Keisha. That's why I'm here. I think she could be the first African American girl gold medalist. In the Olympics, I mean. Her talent is awesome. This summer she'd be on the summer team, traveling with us to do a few meets, not a lot, only one out of Georgia, so she gets used to competing and then when the winter—"

My mama interrupted. "I don't know. I'm not too keen on my kids traveling around and stuff. Would she have to spend the night?"

"Sometimes. This summer maybe only one or two nights at the most. But there's always two women chaperons with the girls. And I'd keep my eye on her personally. God knows I wouldn't want anything to happen to her. I *do* understand what can happen to children."

"I don't know," Mama said again, leaning back now, rubbing her forehead.

"What about you? Would you mind coming along as a chaperon, then?" Mr. Walt said, smiling at Mama. "That way you could be sure she was all right. Believe me, competing is important for her development as a swimmer or I wouldn't ask."

"Well, I don't know. I know I couldn't do it right now because of my working. But maybe later," Mama said, looking at him again. "I tell you what. We can try it. I do trust *you*. I'll see how Keisha likes it. She's never stayed away from home. She might not like it," she said, looking at me.

"I'll like it, Mama," I said. "I want to swim."

"Okay. Okay," she said. shaking her head, "I'll let her go this summer. Maybe I'll even go on a trip."

"Just let me know when," Mr. Walt said, grinning.

I could see he liked Mama. I was wondering if she could see it, too. I thought, Wouldn't it be nice if Mr. Walt fell in love with Mama? But I didn't say it. I didn't want to jinx it. I liked Mr. Walt. He was the nicest man I'd ever known up until this point in my life.

I never knew my father. He left when I was about three years old. Punky is our half brother but we never say that. Mama don't like for you to mention "half whatever." We don't even know who his daddy was because Mama refuses to discuss it. She tells Punky his daddy is dead. But me and Rhenda don't think so. She says our daddy is dead, too. I want to believe he is, since he don't even come to see us. Actually I'd begun to think there were no nice men.

After Mr. Walt left, Mama went straight to bed. I knew why. Not because she was tired but she didn't want to talk about what had happened. Sometimes Mama ignored stuff, like that would make it go away.

I went in our room. Rhenda was knocked out 'sleep on the bed, still hugging Tomika. I lay down across the bed and read a book that Rhenda got for me from the library. She sometimes takes the baby to the library to see the books all stacked in one place. Rhenda thinks I should be a writer and a doctor. Rhenda writes a lot. She's the one should write. But she's got it in her head that her life is supposed to be over except for taking care of Tomika.

The book was written by a black woman named Bell Hooks. I liked this woman—she don't take no shit. She don't let nobody stop her—not fear—not nothing. Yes, the more I read the more I liked this Bell Hooks. I fell asleep dreaming that I was Bell Hooks in a fancy college writing about myself.

When I woke up I went in Mama's room. I sat on the edge of her double bed. "Mama, can I talk to you a minute?"

She turned over, mumbling. I knew she wasn't really 'sleep. Cat breathing could wake her up. She wanted me to go away. She could sense what I was going to ask her. I knew that.

"Mama?"

She sat up. Turned on the light. "Yes, Keisha? What . . . is . . . it?"

The drawn-out "what . . . is . . . it" means she really don't want to talk. "Why you never told me you was smart in school?"

"What good was that going to do?"

"I just want to know, that's all. It helps me to know you were book smart."

She shrugged. "I didn't think it would do you no good, maybe even hurt you in the long run."

"How, Mama? How could my knowing you was smart hurt me? That's a good thing, Mama."

"Maybe. Do you remember when Rhenda was your age?"

"Yes, I remember." I didn't want to, but I did. That's

when she and Mama started yelling with each other all the time.

"Well, I told Rhenda that. She was making good grades, and I told her one time that I'd made good grades just like her when I was her age. But making good grades ain't mean much in the long run if you gon' let boys sniff you up."

"So," I said. "So you told Rhenda. What's wrong with that?"

"Nothing, *I thought*. But you know, after that, I noticed Rhenda started messing up. Messing up at school first, then next thing you know she was pregnant. I don't know how, but somehow I think my telling her that hurt her."

"That doesn't make any sense, Mama."

"I know. But everything ain't gonna make sense that happens. Being a mama is the hardest thing in the world. Ain't nobody tell you nothing 'bout how to do it. I wasn't much older than you when I had Rhenda. I tried to tell her not to have no baby. I say, 'Rhenda, don't you see how hard it is for me?' But, just like me, she hardheaded and wouldn't listen. Now look what's don' happened. I did everything wrong, I guess. Even when you think you doing the right thing, it turns out to be wrong. I don't know. Being a mama is so hard for me."

"You a good mama," I said, wishing now I hadn't brought it up. This kind of talking always made Mama start looking sad for days after. I figured out a while back that's why she don't talk about the old days. The old days hurt her bad.

She hugged me. She grabbed me and hugged me. Mama always hug us a lot. She say her mama didn't never hug her much. I can't see it, though. Grandma hugged us a lot. But maybe Grandma changed when she got older. Seen that a person needed to be hugged. Too bad she ain't know'd it with Mama.

I could feel her crying inside, even though she let go of me and said, "You best go to bed so you can get up in the morning. You know I got to get up in a few hours. I can't sit up talking all night with you, girl. Get on outta here. You know I get stupid if I don't get ten hours' sleep."

Later, I heard her muffled crying.

Me and Rhenda slept in the same room. We had twin beds. Rhenda's baby slept all cuddled up beside her. I wanted to ask Rhenda what happened. Did Mama being smart in school have something to do with her giving up on good grades, running buck wild, and then getting pregnant? But I didn't. I tried reading for a while, but I couldn't keep my mind on the book. I kept reading the same page again and again. Finally, I just turned over and went to sleep.

The next day at swimming Mr. Walt whistled and waved me out of the water. He was talking to the tallest, cutest, big foot man I've ever seen in person. I thought he must be a basketball player. Oh, my God. Maybe he's a *professional* basketball player. I could kill Mr. Walt, I thought, as I felt up to my hair. It was all wild and stuff. Chlorine does a number on black hair. It makes it more wiry and kinky, as my grandma used to call it.

"Yes sir," I said, shivering as I walked toward him and the man, water dripping from the seat of my swimsuit like I was peeing. I hate that. I had forgot my towel downstairs. So I had to shake like a dog to get some of the water off.

The two of them, Mr. Walt and the Giant, were smiling at me. I couldn't look in their faces, I felt so embarrassed, and I wasn't even sure why.

"Here's your surprise, Keisha," Mr. Walt said, beaming like Santa Claus.

"Sir?" I said. Mr. Walt was old fashioned. He wanted us to say sir to him.

"This is Sabir Muhammad. He came all the way from Atlanta to meet you."

I stood there, looking stupid. Who in the world was Sabir Muhammad?

Sabir said, "You don't know who I am. That's okay." He tilted his head. "Mr. Walt tells me you're a natural swimmer. And that you're really smart in school, too. That's great."

"Thanks," I said, shivering.

"Sabir here," Mr. Walt said, "is an Olympic champion, Keisha."

"He is?" I said, like Mr. Walt had just announced this Sabir guy was the president of the United States come to meet me. I ain't never knew no black man won the swimming part of the Olympics. "That's the bomb," I said.

"Whoa. Not yet," Sabir said. "Coach, I mean, Mr. Walt, is jumping the gun here."

"Are you some kind of a scout or agent or something?" I asked.

He shook his head. "I grew up in a neighborhood

much like this one, except in Atlanta. That's where I met Mr. Walt. He used to be my coach. I've not too long ago finished school, but I'm a swimmer, too."

"Where did you go to school?" I asked him. He looked too old for high school.

"I've been in graduate school. Now I'm getting my doctorate."

The minute I heard the word "doctor," he had me.

"Listen to him, Keisha," Mr. Walt said. "He only graduated from Stanford with a four point zero average. He joined the U.S.A. Swimming Resident Team in 1998. He's broken American records five or more times and is currently the seventeenth-fastest man *ever* in the one hundred-meter fly."

Mr. Walt was looking at him like, as my grandma used to say, "He could eat him whole."

Sabir said, "Coach, please. Let it rest."

I wondered why I never heard of this guy.

"Muhammad here," Mr. Walt continued, "was the fourth African American to qualify for a U.S. National team. He was a twenty-four-time all-American at Stanford."

"Okay, Coach," Sabir said. "Let's get back to Keisha. It's not easy to keep up your grades and do all that's required for swimming, but if you want to, it can be done. The training is brutal."

"Training?" I asked him. "Besides swimming?"

"You've got dryland training, weights, exercises, you know, calisthenics, running, jumping rope, stretching—so much to get ready. Competition is fierce."

"Yes, but," Mr. Walt interrupted, "it will help build your concentration and self-esteem, right, Sabir?"

I was beginning to understand why Mr. Walt hadn't mentioned any of this training stuff.

"What's most important is whether you like to swim or not, Keisha," Sabir said.

I stood there for a minute, shivering. Water dripped from the ends of my hair and rolled down my arm like miniature streams. My teeth were chattering. The truth was, I didn't think about it. Swimming left me space not to think. "I guess I love it," I said.

Sabir nodded. "Do you want to compete?" he asked.

Did I? I hadn't thought much about competition, either. I don't know that I'd ever competed for much except maybe who's going to eat the most cake or something like that. Sure, I played pickup and sports, but I didn't really get into the winning thing too much. I just liked playing, you know, moving around, exercising. I shrugged.

"You don't know?" he asked.

"Sure, she knows," Mr. Walt said, like he really knew. "I see you sprinting forward like a bullet in the water when you hear the whistle blow," he said, grinning at me. Then he said to Sabir, "That girl's head comes up out of the water. She might spot Betty there right on her tail in the next lane, or even Swan, and then she just takes off. Don't you?" he asked, looking at me, grinning.

"Yeah. I do that," I said, "but to be honest, I don't know if I ever thought about it."

"Don't worry. That's a good thing," Sabir said. "When

I'm swimming, I'm not swimming so much to win or compete. I just like being fast. Beating my own time. There isn't a thing wrong with that."

Mr. Walt yelled to one of the other kids all laid back in a chair near his desk. "Hey, bring me that towel over there."

The kid ran up and handed Mr. Walt the towel. "Here," he said, handing it to me. "You look like you're cold."

I wrapped the towel around my shoulders. "Thanks, Mr. Walt."

"She'll get that fever. You got it, Sabir," Mr. Walt said. "You don't know it, that's all, Keisha. See, when black folks don't know it and they doing something sometimes it happens like that, *bam*." Mr. Walt slapped his palms together. "Sometimes it happens to women too. *Bam*."

"What?" I said, totally lost.

"That competition thing. You know, it's like Sabir here. He don't admit it, but every time he hear he's the first African American that did so and so, or, that there ain't been one of us in the Olympics to win—something in him goes, 'Oh, I'm gonna do that. Got to.'"

Sabir shrugged like maybe this was Mr. Walt's fantasy and he wasn't in it.

Mr. Walt kept on, "With women, white women athletes, I've seen it. They're figuring, okay, so you kept us out of the Olympics for a while, but now—we gonna whip your butts. And *bam*." Mr. Walt clapped his hands again. "You got, what's her name? You know, Sabir.

86

What's her name?" Mr. Walt said, rubbing his forehead.

Seeing him do that reminded me of Mama. She always rubbed her forehead when she was thinking of something.

Sabir said, "Do you mean Tracy Caulkins?"

"Yeah, that's it," Mr. Walt said. "People say she's the greatest swimmer who ever lived. She's the *only* one ever to own an American record in all the strokes. Ain't no man did that. The woman was sho'nuf bad now."

Sabir said, "I suppose I do try harder since I know it's important for an African American to swim in National competitions or the Olympics. It opens doors for us all. My parents taught me that. But we've got Byron Davis, fastest man in the butterfly, who's about to make it. I'd bet on it."

"Sure, you right," Mr. Walt said, smiling.

"Well, that hasn't happened to me yet," I said. "I like swimming and all. But I want to be a doctor."

"What do you think I brought Sabir here for?" Mr. Walt said. "Ain't nobody smarter than my man here. He could easily be a doctor of medicine if he wanted to. But he's going for that international stuff. Right, Sabir?"

"International communications. And coach is correct. If you study and work hard, you can do both."

I shook my head. "Maybe I'll think about it." Right now, though, I was thinking about how my hair must look to this guy. I don't know why, 'cause Sabir too old for me.

Sabir said, "I've got to run. It was a pleasure meeting you, Keisha." He reached for my hand. With both of his. "I hope to see you compete one day. Maybe by February you'll be ready for the Black History Invitational Swim meet. I'll be there this year."

"What is that?" I asked him, realizing his hands were softer than my own.

Mr. Walt said, "She'll be there. Count on it. And she's going to blow 'em out of the water. Tracy Caulkins, look out."

Sabir said, "It's a swim meet where all the black swimmers can get together and meet each other. And compete, too. It's fun; you get a lot of exposure to other black swimmers. Most of the time when you're doing meets you're not going to meet a lot of us, particularly in Nationals. But hopefully that's changing. Right, Coach?"

"She'll be there. Won't you, Keisha?" he said, as though we'd already discussed it and made a plan.

"I might," I said. "But first I've got to get into Avery."

"Avery University?" Sabir asked. "I thought you were just going to the tenth grade."

"I am, but they have a program for minority students. It begins in the summer but goes half days during school."

"Sounds great. Remember, no one can stop you from doing what you want to do except you, yourself. Coach taught me that."

Mr. Walt smiled and looked down.

God, I thought. The man's blushing.

Sabir shook my hand again. "Great to meet you."

"Good to meet you, too," I said as he walked away talking to Coach.

I went downstairs to shower. Betty was sitting on the bench.

"What are you doing here?" I asked her. "I thought you left early."

"I'm waiting on you. I need to go with you home today. If it's okay."

"Sure. We can listen to music. Rhenda's got some new recipe, though, so if it don't work out, we might have to eat beans or something."

"I don't care," Betty said. "It's cool."

I showered and started dressing. I didn't even bother to comb my hair. It was a mess. That is the one thing I hate about swimming. Your hair don't never look right. It bothered me that all Clarissa had to do was shake hers out and it looked fine. In fact, even wet it looked okay. She could make me sick sometimes.

Betty didn't care, 'cause her hair was closer to Clarissa's, what we call "good hair." Mama say all hair is good. Betty was sitting now, leaning back, chillin' like she always does, waiting for me to finish up. Betty would help me untangle my hair.

I didn't ask her why she wanted to come with me home. She was my best friend now. And you should not bug your best friend unless you got good reason. At least, that's the way it is with me and Rhenda.

I told Miss Troutman about the swim team the next morning. I explained to her that I'd have to go five days a week instead of three days. And I'd have to stay most of the day. She complained that I might miss too much time from the at-risk program, specifically the at-risk program's girl's basketball team. The team Kimmie girl had just started.

Miss Troutman said Kimberly was counting on me to help her with the team.

"But that's not what *I* want to do," I protested. "She don' already told me she don't know nothing 'bout basketball, so how she gon' coach somebody?" I didn't add that I didn't want to be on no team miss high-and-mighty, nose-up-in-the-air Kimmie girl was coaching. It didn't take no psychic network to know we couldn't get along. I could tell by the way she constantly rolled her eyes at me that I wasn't exactly her favorite person in the world.

Miss Troutman said, "First of all, that is why Kimberly feels she needs your assistance on the team, Keisha. But either way, I'll have to check with Mr. Pierce. We have a plan to follow. To be honest, this whole swimming thing was not a part of our plans. We have to send two counselors over to the pool each time. And Clarissa is always late coming back with the van. I just don't know. So don't get your hopes up. Now, I have paperwork to do," she said, and bent her head down to her desk.

I knew that meant the talk was over.

As soon as I stepped out of the office, Clarissa walked up to me. "What did she say?"

"About what?"

"Your being on the swim team. Mr. Walt told me he'd asked you."

I thought to myself, Does she know *all* my business? "She said she'd have to think about it, is what she said. Which probably means no."

"Oh, yeah? Come with me," Clarissa said, taking me by the hand. She pulled me back into Miss Troutman's office.

"Excuse me, Miss Troutman," Clarissa began. "Could I say something, please?"

Miss Troutman looked up. "Yes?" Then she glanced back to her papers.

I couldn't help but smile a little because I could see Miss Troutman wasn't as racist as I thought. She was still reading her papers the same way she'd done when I was in the office alone.

"I've seen Keisha swim, and she is really good. I hope she's going to be on that swim team. I don't mind going over there with her every day to practice. And since it's just a few of the kids instead of all eleven I can do it by myself. Kimmie won't have to go. It's kind of fun, really. Plus, you've got to see Keisha swim."

Miss Troutman looked up and laid her pen down. "Didn't she just *learn* to swim since she's been going over there?"

"Yes," Clarissa said, "but she could outswim me by the second day. She's like a dolphin in the water, Miss Troutman. You have to see it to believe it."

"Well, I suppose it won't hurt . . . "

I couldn't close my mouth. I had this funny feeling inside, remembering all the bad thoughts I'd had about Clarissa.

As we walked out I brushed up against old stuck-up Kimmie. She must have been right outside the door.

Kimmie quickly jumped back like I'd electrocuted her. I kept walking but I heard her behind me, saying, "Excuse me, Miss Troutman. I have something very important to talk with you about."

Suddenly I felt happy again. I thanked Clarissa but didn't know what else to say to her. I wanted to say more, but what?

She stood still for a minute, like maybe she didn't

know what to say either, other than, "You're welcome." And then she bit her bottom lip and walked away.

I leaned up against the wall, sighing with relief. Maybe I should have thanked Miss Troutman for saying yes and recognizing how important this swim team was to me. That was it.

I turned around and headed back. When I got to the office, the door was closed. I stood outside, considering whether I should knock.

The sound of Kimmie's voice inside was clear, "I think it's, like, a bad idea to let the kids do what they want to do. Like, after all, like the whole point of them being here is to teach them to respect authority, like follow a routine, and establish, like, responsible behavior. Plus, like, Keisha is good at *basketball*. I can't handle this team all by myself."

I could hear Miss Troutman's response: "Keisha doesn't want to play basketball. She wants to swim. Clarissa says she's good at that, too."

"Yeah, well like, I have been reluctant to bring this up, but Keisha has, like, an attitude problem since she's been attending those swimming sessions. She, like, always has to have the last word, and, like, she's talking when she's not called upon. Like she started telling the other kids to try things, even before we've decided what they're like supposed to do next. I just think, like this swimming thing is a bad idea.

"And the old black man, well, he's like always touching her. I don't mean to imply that they are like having any kind of an affair. But I think that maybe . . . like, do you know what I'm saying here? This is so, like, embarrassing."

I couldn't believe what I was hearing.

Miss Troutman said, "Oh. So that's why she's dying to go over there every day. Well, I suspected this might become one of our problems with these children. You see, Kimberly, I know you're an African American, but you come from a different background. You've had opportunities they will never have, and I'm sure you don't really understand how different you are from them. But hopefully you won't let them influence you negatively. I've heard how in black communities some children discourage others from learning."

"I do understand, Miss Troutman. Like, that's exactly why I'm telling you this. If that girl Kaneisha, like, wants to make something of herself, she should like be on our basketball team. After all, like, they have professional women's team that make like loads of money. But like, there's no swimming team that makes any money. I just think that if we can—"

"Well, I'm sorry, but I've already told her that she can be on the swimming team. Clarissa volunteered to go over with them every day."

"Clarissa? She doesn't, like, know anything about poor black people. I don't mean, like, any harm but, like, she's white. Plus, I think she just, like, wants to be liked. In fact, I think she likes black boys. I saw her hugging that Malik Shabazz, like, right in front of everyone. And you know she could, like, be afraid to cross her or something. I heard that Keleisha has, like, a temper. Didn't she, like, jump on a teacher and the principal or something at her school?"

"That's not exactly how it happened, but let's get back to that older man. What is it you think he is doing?"

"Mr. Walt . . . like, that's what he tells the little girls to call him. Like, his name is Walter Bullock. But, like, he tells them to, like, call him *Mr. Walt*."

"Yes, but have you ever seen this Mr. Walt, well . . . you know, touch Keisha inappropriately?"

"I don't, like, want to be a snitch, but—"

They got quiet. Whispering now. I couldn't make out what they were saying. I wanted to burst in the room and hurt somebody, well not somebody, that Kimmie girl specifically, and hurt her bad.

So I took off running. Sweat poured down my face with my tears. My hair stuck to my forehead. I jumped on the city bus looking like a dog caught in a storm. I wanted to be home with my mama.

She would know what to do. She always knew what to do. White people think black people's mamas don't know nothing. But my mama knows, even if she ain't set foot in no college. Even if she ain't got no GED. My mama is smart. Mr. Walt said so. And, one thing is for sure I know, my mama always takes care of her kids.

The next morning when I came to the SCARF
center, my mama was with me. We took the city bus.
When we got there, she walked up to Miss Troutman,
right up in her face, and said, "I want to talk to you."

Miss Troutman backed a few feet away like Mama's
breath might stink.

But Mama had kissed me on the cheek just before we
came through the door, so I knew her breath didn't smell
bad.

Miss Troutman turned and said, "Miss Wright, please
follow me into *my* office. I'm sure there's a good reason
why Keisha missed the minibus this morning. She's been

doing very well so far catching it on time. And I'm not surprised that now after a few weeks she's getting a little lazy. But I do need to speak with you about another matter."

My mama didn't say anything. She just took my hand, and we walked in the office together.

Miss Troutman said, "Please have a seat," and she walked around the desk and sat down in her high-back leather swivel chair. She picked up her fountain pen and began tapping the highly polished wooden desk. She cleared her throat and said, "It is not easy to teach children, and sometimes even the parents, the importance of being on time. *We* understand. You see, I am aware of the idea that because your roots are in Africa, you may not see time in a linear fashion as we do. And I'm sure that's because harvesting is not done according to a clock," she said, smiling.

I thought to myself, What in the heck is she rambling about now? This women is whacked.

She nodded her head like she knew what she'd just said was a fact that had something to do with us. Then she continued. "So we do expect to make exceptions for our black, I mean, excuse me, African American children. You see, in this program we respect your heritage." Miss Troutman leaned back in her chair, then crossed her legs at the knee.

My mama said, "What did you say your name was?"

"Oh, I'm sorry. I assumed Keisha had provided you my name. It's Miss Troutman. But you may call me Gayle." She had pulled out a folder and looked inside. "And I'll call you . . . Carolyn. How about that?"

My mama stared at her for a moment and then said, "I think I'll just stick with Miss Troutman. And you can stick to Mrs. Wright. How about that?"

My mama didn't crack a smile.

Miss Troutman squirmed in her seat. "Sure. No problem," she said. "Anyway, as I was saying—"

Mama held up her palm toward Miss Troutman. "Miss, did you come to my house to see me?" Mama asked, still not smiling.

"Well no," Miss Troutman said, fidgeting in her chair, while looking inside the folder like her answers might be written on paper. "No," she stammered, "don't worry, we do plan to have a parenting workshop before the end of the summer. We just haven't found a trained therapist to conduct it yet. But we're working on it. And as soon as we're ready we will notify you."

My mama smiled and said, "Miss Troutman. I came here to see you. In my neighborhood that means I have something to say. What does it mean in yours?"

"Oh, my. Of course, forgive me. Of course. Go right ahead. Please."

My mama rolled her eyes into the top of her head. "Look, my daughter tells me somebody here has been lying on her. And I need to get to the bottom of this before I have to go off on somebody up in here. Do you understand what I'm talking about?"

"Why, no. *Excuse me*. Oh. Actually, I might know. Would you excuse us, Keisha. This is a delicate matter and I'd like to speak to your mother alone."

I stood up, but Mama pulled me back down by my

shirttail. "If this involves Keisha, she needs to hear it, miss. I don't keep nothing from my kids. So spit it out whatever it is you got to say."

She don't? I thought. Mama know she exaggerating.

"Well, Miss Wright . . . I think—"

"Mrs. Wright," my mama said, and stared at Miss Troutman like she was an animal in the zoo. The same way Miss Troutman had been looking at us.

"Sure. Mrs. Wright, I'm sorry," Miss Troutman said. "I'll get right to the point. In fact, I'd considered calling the police today about this. But I wanted to make sure it was a nonconsensual experience. You see, I believe that someone has been molesting your daughter."

"Who?" my mama asked calmly.

"Well, I can't speak for anything that might have happened in the past. I know how this type of thing happens in your neighborhoods, but more recently I think it is an older black man who has been coercing her into swimming for the express purpose of fondling— are you sure you want me to continue *in front of your child?*"

My mama frowned up. "It seems to me if somebody been feeling on my girl, she already know it, so what could you be saying that would be news to her, miss?"

"I see," Miss Troutman said icily, turning the color of cherry Kool-Aid. "Maybe you don't understand the sensitivity in which this subject must—"

"What I understand is you telling me . . . you think somebody bothered my daughter. And I want to know who it is and why you thinking it? And even more so, I want to know why in the hell you would think she wouldn't tell me if it were true?"

"Miss Wright, there is no need for profanity here. I'm on your side."

"Are you? And I ain't telling you no more it's Mrs., either. Okay?" my mama said, folding her hands in her lap. Now she leaned back in her chair.

"Many children," Miss Troutman said, almost in tears, "who have been molested by a family member or friend find it difficult, if not impossible, to tell their parent. The perpetrator, that is the person who molested her—"

"I watch television, miss. I know what a perpetrator is. It's a black man, isn't it?"

"Oh, you misunderstand. I'm not implying that all black men are perpetrators, Mrs. Wright. Statistically I could make that case, but . . . "

I could tell my mama was tired now. Her shoulders straightened. She leaned in toward the desk, gripping the chair arm, and said, "Let's cut to the chase. I know my daughter well. She knows me. We have a close relationship. If any man, father, brother, friend, neighbor, you name it touched her, I'd cut their dick off and serve it to them for breakfast. Now if you think that she's been molested, I want to know how you got this idea? And I want you to quit wasting time, because I've been up half the night working and I'm tired. I don't have time for no more bullshit."

Miss Troutman lowered her voice to almost a whisper. "Well, one of my counselors had been noticing this older black man named Walter, the kids call him Mr. Walt, taking up a lot of time with your daughter. And last evening she described to me a scene she witnessed last week, where she came over to the pool and found your daughter, Keisha, sitting with her legs sprawled open, and this man, Walt, rubbing her thighs."

"Uh-huh. And who is it that told you this?"

"That doesn't matter. What you need to be concerned about is your daughter, Mrs. Wright." The tears had vanished from Miss Troutman's eyes, and something more like being mad was showing 'cause my mama had the nerve to be talking back to her.

My mama stood up. She walked around to the side of the desk.

Miss Troutman reached out for the phone receiver.

My mama said in a low, soft voice, "What you should be concerned about is a *lying* counselor, miss. My daughter caught a cramp. Keisha told me about that when it happened. Mr. Walt lifted her out of the pool and massaged her thigh. Then he sent me a note asking me to make sure Keisha increased her potassium and magnesium intake to help her with leg cramps in the water. The cramp was in her thigh. What do you suggest he do—rub her forehead?

"Now that's it. Mr. Walt has never done nothing but be nice to Keisha. He even came to my house to ask my permission for her to be on the swim team and go to the swim meets. That's more than y'all ever done. He even wanted me to go to the meets with them, so I could be one of the chaperons. I suppose so he could mess with me, too. But I couldn't because I work.

"So, now I'm only going to say this once, miss whatever your name is, if I hear another damn word about my daughter that is not the honest-to-God truth, somebody up in here is going to be sorry. And I don't mean me. Do you get my drift here, Miss Troutman?"

Miss Troutman shook her head up and down and stared at the phone. Her tears were back.

My mama continued, "And I ain't talking about coming up here raising hell or fighting. I'm not the Jerry Springer type. I'm talking about taking your asses to court for defamation of my daughter's character." And with that, Mama marched out with me right behind her.

I didn't know for sure why that Kimmie girl told this lie on me. Maybe if I hadn't overheard her she would have finally convinced Miss Troutman to make me play basketball. God, did she want to win the basketball summer tournament so she could show off to her boyfriend that bad? Well, now there's no way in hell I'd play. I couldn't believe she actually thought there was something happening between me and Mr. Walt. I planned to ask her about it, but Mama said forget about the nut and go on and swim like a fish.

In the pool I *was* a fish. I glided smooth through the water, and the world was silent and warm. When my head sunk below the surface, I was in a cocoon. I could close my eyes and I'd be in space, not thinking—just free—totally free.

I dived and hit the water barely making a splash; it stung for a second, but then I was shooting through the water swimming, gliding, a butterfly soaring free again. I was a fish. A very, very fast fish.

Malik watched me today dive from the board.

When I came out of the water he was kneeling where I pulled up. I was embarrassed because I was wearing an ugly swim cap. But that was better than him seeing my hair.

"Hey, good dive," he said, grinning.

"Thanks," I said, blushing, glad that because of my color, he couldn't tell it.

Mr. Walt came over. "Hey, Keisha. Great dive. Pretty soon you'll be better than old Malik here. Malik, are you going with us Saturday? It's the girls' first official meet outside this league. They'll be competing against a tough group in Alabama. You can come if you want."

I held my breath. I wanted him to come and I didn't want him to.

"Naw," Malik said. "I've been asked to go somewhere Saturday with Clarissa."

I stopped breathing and dived back in the water. I swam to the bottom of the pool and sat with my legs crossed. I wanted to stay there until hell froze over, like my grandma used to say.

But too quickly Betty was down there pulling on me to come up. When we were resting on the side of the pool, our feet dangling in the water, she said, "What's up with you? Why you trippin'?"

"Nothing. I'll be okay," I said. I wanted to tell her I liked her brother, but if I said it out loud, then I could never take it back. So I just hopped up, dried off with a towel, and walked out to the van. I'd shower later at the center.

Some girls are fast early. Not me. My mama don' told me it's better to learn how to take care of your own body. I'm supposed to be able to please myself until I'm grown or at least out of high school. She said that's why the Surgeon General of the United States, Dr. Joycelyn Elders, got fired. Because she was a practical black woman trying to teach young girls, especially black girls, to give themselves their own pleasure. Instead, the white folks, who always crying about us having babies, let her go. Fired her and said, "Don't tell them that." But Mama said it's something girls need to know. Then they won't have to have no boy too early. "Masturbation could have been your sister's lifesaver, if I'd had sense enough to tell her earlier," Mama said.

My mama also cautioned me that love and sex ain't the same. "Just 'cause some hardhead boy say he love you, don't mean a thing. Just tell him you love him, too, but he ain't getting none. You' gon' have to learn to love yourself first, and then boys. Otherwise you gon' be as confused as I was," she said. "When I was your age I was thinking magic stuff. You know, like if you pray hard enough or don't think about it, you won't get pregnant. Bull. If you open your legs, something gon' go in and nine months later somebody gon' come out."

My mama don't take no stuff off men. But she still like 'em, though. She said a whole woman can find a whole man if she looking in the right place. She said a young girl just gon' end up with a young boy and that means y'all ain't ready for much more than a good kiss.

I've let a boy kiss me a little, but I ain't never been with a boy and I ain't ashamed of that. And I never wanted to be with one, really, until the day I saw Malik rubbing his sister's forehead. I don't know why, but something about the way he was doing that reached inside me and touched me. That don't mean I'd be stupid enough to do nothing, though.

Of course, I ain't tell nobody. Not even Betty. Me and her, we swim together always. We take turns following in each other's wake. I swim ahead and use the rippling water like a propeller pulling me forward, and sometimes she's in front. Mr. Walt says it doesn't really make us go any faster, but we think it does.

Betty is a good swimmer, too. Not better than me but a whole lot braver than me. Because I don't know if I would ever swim if I'd almost drowned. She ain't dumb, either. We been studying together two nights a week. Usually when she comes over to help me with my hair from swimming I ask her to help me study. She thinks I'm doing it just for me. But, naw, I want us both to do good.

At first she said, she don't want to be smarter. She ain't no white girl.

Then I told her what Mr. Hakim said about being smart ain't come from no white people.

Betty asked her uncle, who is a Rasta, and he told her me and Mr. Hakim are right. He told her that white people want people to believe they invent learning. That they set the standard for what's right in the world. But he's read the great history of the Egyptians, the Nubians, the Kushites, the Japanese, and the Chinese. These people been learning long before any white man come along. So she told me this and started studying with me.

Whenever I would ask her anything about Malik, she

just start giggling. She said, "Malik don't much care for girls."

One night when he come to walk Betty home, I asked my mama if that meant Malik was gay.

My mama said she don't know, but if he is he is sho'nuf cute to be gay.

When I got outside I saw Clarissa talking to Malik by the minibus. As usual they were standing real close. I yanked open the van door and plopped down inside. My mama has this saying, when she sees a black guy with a white girl, "Show a black man a white woman, and you might as well go on and hang him, because he gonna keep on messing with her until somebody jacks him up." I wanted to cry, but my mama said I'm too young to start crying over boys. She said they gonna make me cry in plenty of time, so don't rush it.

I was glad when Betty came out, because Malik moved away from Clarissa and got on the bus. He sat on the last seat and laid his head back.

I rubbed my hair. It felt rough and I could see my reflection in the van's window. Swimming and my hair wasn't gon' mix. If I want Malik maybe I'm gon' have to stop this swimming. The thought made my stomach lurch. "If I want Malik." Where did that come from? Do I like him? Shit, yeah. I might as well go on and 'fess up. I got to tell somebody. I feel like singing now that I can think it out loud in my mind. I *do* like Malik. But then when it was his turn to get off the van I saw him stop and hand Clarissa a notebook.

Darn. Did he buy her a notebook?

She gathered her blond hair up in her hands and then flipped it back.

Malik grinned and stepped off the van.

I wanted to hit her. Or have her hair, one.

Saturday was the swim meet in Alabama. Mama fussed over me leaving like I was a soldier going to war. She packed me sandwiches and kept asking me to check to make sure I had everything. She must have asked me a kazillion times, "Are you sure you're gonna be all right?"

Rhenda wasn't much better. She gave me one of Tomika's old rattles to take for good luck.

Punky was the only one acting like I was going overnight to a swim meet. He just said, "Break a bubble." Sometimes he kills me.

I had never stayed in a hotel before. It was fun. We ate pizza, danced, and did our nails.

At the meet, I was nervous like a mouse at a cat's party.

Betty was pacing back and forth like a tiger in a cage, but she said she was cool.

Mr. Walt forgot to tell us one little minor detail about our competition. They were all white girls. Thin, skinny-legged white girls with fancy Speedo caps and matching flowered bathing suits and thongs on their feet. They strutted around laughing and squealing like this was their world and they was just loaning us the air we breathed in it.

The meet was being held at this exclusive country club. I wasn't scared of white people, but sometimes, whether I could admit it or not, they make me feel funny. "Funny" isn't the right word. The word is "inadequate." Sometimes, I think as much as I fight it, I might believe all the ugly things white people say about black people. Not all the time, but in times like these, I'm not so sure of myself. Especially when I know we're someplace that they don't even let black people or Jewish people join. I don' already overheard coach talking about it. How they probably hurtin' 'cause we here.

Even the decorations make me feel uncomfortable. At the side of the pool, they had a large table with a white linen cloth draping it with real live flowers sitting on each end, a big old ice sculpture of a swan melting fast in the center. There were waiters with trays serving every-one. The girls' parents were all sitting around in fancy curved chairs, sipping wine in real wineglasses, everybody dressed in name-brand stuff. The women were wearing gold-and-diamond tennis bracelets. Not the thin kind I normally see but big old sparkling diamonds big as cornflakes. They got pearls 'round their necks, too. It wasn't escaping me that when they looked at us, they seem to cringe.

One of the girls walked over to me. She had her nose turned up like we smelled. "Hi," she said. "We were wondering, are you girls wearing swimming caps in our pool?"

I couldn't answer. Why would she ask me that?

Betty overheard her and answered, "Why you asking? What's it to you?"

Betty didn't tolerate white people as well as I did. She believed them to always be up to no good.

"Betty," I said, trying to lighten her up, "maybe they want to know if our team caps are matched colors, you know, all the same like theirs?" I was hoping the girl would just walk away before she got Betty started.

"Well, we have a rule," the girl continued, "that you have to wear swim caps to be in the pool, that's all."

"What about her?" Betty asked, pointing.

There was a white girl with long brunette hair swimming laps in the ten-feet section of the pool. No cap.

"She's a member here."

Betty sneered at her. "So what you saying is you want to know if us black girls is wearing caps?"

"No," the girl began stuttering. "I don't mean . . . well, it's just that, we don't usually have outsiders. I mean people."

"Go ahead," Betty said, closing in on her and spitting

the words out like they were equivalent to snake venom. "You mean black people."

By this time two more white girls had come over but they hadn't said anything.

Trying my best to smile, I said, "Sure. We always wear our caps to swim. No problem." I held my white Speedo up so they could see it.

The three girls quickly moved away.

"Bitches," Betty said.

Betty didn't mind cursing, anytime, anywhere.

"Don't start nothing, okay?" I said, shaking out my legs. "Let's just swim and go home."

"Hey, I didn't start it. If she hadn't come over here I wouldn't have said nothing. Now I'm kicking her ass."

"Betty. You can't go around fighting. They think that's all we know how to do. Why confirm what *they* think about us?"

"I don't give a shit about what *they* think. But I wasn't talking about fighting-fighting. We're busting their butts 'cause we're taking all the trophies home with us, girl-friend." She whistled to our other team members, and said, "We got some asses to whip."

Betty didn't have to explain the meaning of the question the white girl had asked. We knew. We'd witnessed it before when we swam at a white pool in the suburbs near Seward. It was like the white people thought our skin flaked off in the water. Or maybe the grease from our hair would skim the top. We don't hardly use grease anymore, but what do they know? Or maybe they thought that we do something more than just pee in a pool.

Nobody ever came right out and said it, but even when you're little you learn the silent language of what some white people are thinking just by how they're looking at you. There's no hiding from it. You know Jewish people get some of it. Gay people, too. Even other minorities, but they don't have it like we do 'cause they can hide sometimes. They can keep their mouths shut, and their hands to themselves, and nobody knows the difference. Most often, though, there ain't no hiding if you black.

Coach came over and said, "Keisha, see that girl with the white band on her wrist. She's the girl they been talking about. Just be cool. She's pretty fast. She's been swimming for a long time and she's got good technique. All we want is for you to stay close and not worry about it."

I nodded and shook my legs out again.

The whistle blew a shrill note for us to get ready. The seven of us slipped on our different-colored Speedo caps. We were barefoot, so we didn't have to kick off no flip-flops.

We lined up on the racing stands, a white girl in between each one of us. Fourteen lanes, all doing the 100-meter freestyle. We only had a five-lane pool at the MLK Center.

The white girl next to me smiled and waved a tiny wave.

I waved back. She wasn't with those *other* girls. She'd walked away from them just before they came over. I could tell when somebody didn't agree with something but they didn't know what to do about it. I smiled at her to let her know I understood she wasn't with them all the way. I knelt down and breathed a few extra breaths to get ready. I felt my stomach knot up. I might split the water before the whistle went off at this rate. I stood back up and stretched, then shook my legs out one last time, praying I didn't get a cramp.

When the whistle sounded, I forgot everything. I dived. I was swimming inside my mother's womb, trying to get to the light. Trying to get outside to breathe. My lungs burned, but I kept moving my arms in the rhythm that Mr. Walt had taught me. Move your arms to your heartbeat, he said. Keep a smooth flow, don't waste energy, don't look around, swim as straight as you can to your mark. You are a fish in water. You are born in water. You are the water. You are the fish. When I came up I knew I had won. I was first. Betty second. It was the start of a Boston, like in Bid Weis, a card game my mama loves to play. A Boston is when your side wins all the hands. The prim and prissy white girls could kiss our you-know-whats. Before it was over I swept the number one spot in every event.

My only regret was that Mama wasn't there to see it. Maybe next time Mama can chaperon.

It was just six weeks since school let out, and we were smoking everybody. Mr. Walt said me and Betty were going to snatch a spot on the Nationals team and go all the way to the Olympics. I believed him.

Betty didn't. She couldn't shake all that nagging crap about where we were bound to end up. One day she came to swim class with a gold necklace around her neck. I said, "Where you get that? You didn't steal it, did you?"

I had hurt her. She didn't steal. "I'm sorry. It just looks so expensive," I said. "It's pretty. Now tell me"—I tried to sound more happy for her—"where'd you get it?"

"If I tell you, you ain't gon' tell nobody. I mean no-body? Not even your mama?"

"No. Not even my mama."

"And you ain't go freak out, either?"

"Why would I freak out?"

"Just say you are or you ain't?"

"I won't freak out."

"Jeebie gave it to me last night."

"Jeebie?" I spun around on the locker room floor, holding my hands up to my head as though a sharp pain had just struck me. "What Jeebie?"

"You freaking out," she said.

"Jeebie is old enough to be your daddy. And he ain't got that name for nothing. He's a jeeb. He's dangerous and he's a fool. You the one ought to be freaking out."

"Look, I want to have nice things. Don't you see these white girls' stuff? They have on real diamonds and they the same age as us. You think I'm gonna die and have nothing ever to show for it. I ain't dumb like I used to be, thanks to you. I want to have some class. I want the better stuff in life just like the white people got."

"Yeah? You stupid. This ain't nothing about no white people. You gon' get hurt. Jeebie don't respect no woman. He call women bitches and hos and you know it. Why you doing this?"

"What else I'm gon' do? It's easy for you. I ain't gonna go to no college. My mama don't care 'bout me no more—she on drugs. You don't never say it, but I know you know it. We been pretending this summer that if I learn more, things gonna change. Don't you get it?

Nothing really changes for us. Not black people. My mama says it every day. My stepdaddy says it when he drunk. The white man got everything and he gonna keep everything."

"You said it yourself. You gonna listen to a drugged person and a drunk person? That's who you gon' listen to?"

"You rather I listen to Miss Troutman? Mr. Pierce? They don't care nothing 'bout us. This is their *thing*. Their way of making themselves feel better. We their pets, girlfriend. We their save-the-animals-for-the-week project. We ain't nothing but cats and dogs to them."

"So we don't have to rely on them. We have each other."

"You can go to college. Your mama, she gon' go up there when school start and show her behind if they don't turn you back to the college thing. Everybody in that school that's black know that. My mama—she just gon' show her behind, on the street."

"And what you think gon' happen with you and Jeebie?"

"I been seeing Jeebie for a while. Just before school let out. Ain't no thing, you know what I mean. I give him what he want and he give me what I want." She held up her necklace.

"Look," I pleaded. "You pretty, Betty. Everybody think you look good. You ain't got to go there. You can get down with somebody better'n Jeebie. God, girl. That skank. What you want with that fool?"

"You don't know Jeebie like I do. He ain't so bad.

Plus, I ain't seen no Ivy Leaguers hitting on me. White boys don't hit, and black ones all after the same thing Jeebie after, 'cept they ain't got no wad. So if I'm gon' give it away might as well make somebody pay."

I held my palm up to her. "Step off," I said. "I can't deal with you right now."

She shrugged and walked away.

I went home. I caught the city bus instead of waiting for Clarissa. I needed to get as far away from Betty as I could. I couldn't bear to be with her acting so stupid. I left her there hugging that chain to her neck and grinning, while the other girls looked at it like it was a big old steak and they were wild dogs who ain't never ate no food.

That evening when I got home I found my letter from Avery. I read it a thousand times—well, it seemed like a thousand times. The letter said I needed to bring my parent to the interview. Mama coming was not the problem. Since I was no longer eligible through my schoolprogram, I needed to bring my deposit with me. Five hundred dollars! My heart sank. Where was I going to get that kind of money? And in three days?

My mama couldn't work more than 25–30 hours a week at her maid's job no matter what. She made $3.10 an hour plus tips. In a dive motel where mostly migrant workers and prostitutes stay, there's not a lot of tips. I felt like crying as I read the letter. I hadn't thought about the money. I couldn't even remember if Ms. Oliver explained anything about it to me. Maybe there was a mistake. I found Ms. Oliver's number in the phone book.

I read the letter to her over the phone. I asked, "Have they made some mistake?"

"I'm sorry, Keisha," she said. "I didn't explain about the money before because it didn't matter. As long as you were enrolled in college prep you were eligible for a 'learning grant.' After you were switched, I suppose the grants foundation automatically denied your recommendation."

"Can't you change it?" I asked her.

"Keisha. This goes no further than the two of us. Okay?"

"All right."

"I'm not coming back to Primm. I got in a little hot water for signing you up for Avery without discussing it with any school authority. The recommendations were supposed to be done by the guidance counselors. But when I saw that no one from Primm High had been recommended, I just felt I had to put in your name. I shouldn't have done it that way. But when I brought up the deadlines to Ms. Hill, she dismissed recommending anyone from Primm. I made a mistake. I should have convinced her to do it, or approached the principal. And now *you're* having to pay for it."

I felt like throwing up. "It's okay. It doesn't matter. I understand," I said, nearly crying, not sure whether the hurt I heard in her voice was over what happened to me or what had happened to her. I added, "I hope you don't feel bad for having confidence in a student, Ms. Oliver."

"Of course I don't feel bad. I'm fine," she said. "But it did help me decide that it was time for me to leave. I've been reassigned. Actually, I didn't realize you'd continued with the application. That's really good. Does your mother have the money?"

"You mean the deposit?"

"No, I mean the tuition money. I'm sure Avery's already given out the scholarships for next year's programs. I'm sorry, but if I'm not mistaken, you'll have to pay the full tuition."

"You mean it's more than the deposit?" Of course. Why would they need a deposit if there wasn't more money to come? My heart sank to my feet. Here I was worried about the deposit.

"The tuition for the first year is around six thousand dollars. After that you can probably qualify with your good grades for the other two years of high school."

"Six thousand dollars?" I whispered into the phone. I wanted to die. Right then. There was no hope. I would not go to Avery. Probably not medical school, either. All this time I'd just been worried about my grades. Not money, just grades. I assumed that somebody would see how smart I was and give me the money. What a dummy I'd been.

"Listen," Ms. Oliver said, "I'll call around to see if I can find out if there's any money left. But I must tell you, Keisha, I doubt I can find you any for this year. Maybe you'll be able to find another program that's similar. Not

Avery's medical school program, of course, but some other college early-entry program your senior year. Use your Hope scholarship in a state school."

"I want Avery. I'll need their program to pay for medical school. The Avery program is from sophomore to senior in order to qualify for the medical school's tuition to be waived for your first year?" I asked her. "Is that right?"

"Yes, that's what it says."

"I have to go this year, either this summer or during the school term, then. What if my mama gets me back in the college prep classes when school starts? Will that work?"

"I don't think so, Keisha. If you're not signed up by the end of August, you can't go this year and even if you manage to get signed up, your mother would have to have the money. Do you think she could get a loan?"

"That's real funny," I said, hating that I was sounding sarcastic toward her. It wasn't her fault.

"If I had the money, Keisha, I'd give it to you. But I'm pregnant. And my husband's a teacher at Gullat. It's a good school, but the money's the same as at Primm—not very much."

"Don't worry about it. You tried, Ms. Oliver," I said. "Okay. Thanks." What could I do? Nothing. I was glad Mama read the mail early in the morning before she left for work. She didn't see the letter, and I wasn't going to show it to her. Why make her feel bad? Even if she could scrape up the deposit—then what? No. I could just forget about Avery. What made me think I could become a doctor, anyway?

Later, I sat on the bed fiddling with my watch. It was

old and the second hand wasn't working. I looked at that hand while the big hands moved slowly by it, so slow that you couldn't really see the movement. But the next thing you knew, a minute had passed. That was my life. The world was the face of my watch. The big hands were the "other" people, and then there was me. Only I could fix that second hand.

My chest tightened. It hurt. This really hurt. I wanted to scream, but Rhenda and Tomika lay in their bed snoring. I could take a walk. Sneak out.

I listened to make sure Mama was asleep, too. I tiptoed out the back door and ran down the street a ways. I turned left, walked a block. I crossed the street. As I walked, I thought, What could I do to make money? Should I give up? Everything was working against me. I wanted to cry, but I couldn't. What good would it do?

"Hey, Little Sister," Jeebie yelled out his car window. "Hmmm. You sho' look good to me."

That man is like roaches. He is everywhere he ain't supposed to be.

I walked faster. I could take off running back home if he stopped the car.

"Hey, you. Hold it right there," a man's voice boomed.

Jeebie sped off, tires squealing.

Thank God, *the police*. But, I didn't see anyone and I began to feel uneasy. I heard the voice closer now.

"Hey, you better get your little fast-tail butt home."

I strained to see who it was. Only Grandma ever called me "fast-tail." I couldn't see anyone.

I could run. But the voice had come from the direction

of home. I know, I'd sprint past him so fast, he wouldn't have a chance to grab me. I took a deep breath. Then I saw a shadow. A man's figure loomed ahead behind a bush. He wobbled and fell over, out of sight.

A drunk, I thought, letting out a sigh. I could handle him. Probably one of the old winos who hang out up at the store.

The man jumped out at me. "Mama gon' whup your butt for being out here, girl."

"Punky," I yelled, stumbling backwards. "You scared the shit out of me."

"Then there won't be none left for Mama to beat out of you. You know you gon' get it, don't you?"

"What are you doing here?" I said, patting my heart with my hand to calm down. "You the one gon' get it, scaring me like that."

"Girl, I saved your little behind, didn't I?" he said, grinning. "Or did you want to do the *nasty* with old Funk Master Jeeb?"

"Come on, let's go home," I said, smacking him playfully on the head. "You fool."

"You got that right. I almost broke my neck standing up on them cardboard boxes. Good thing they didn't cave in when the Funk Monster was around. He'd a caught me—and run me out of town." We both broke out laughing. "Why you here walking around in Bab-be-lon?" he asked, using his fake Jamaican accent.

"You better quit hanging out with that Rasta boy," I said, mockingly. "You sounding just like him."

"Better him than the Jeebs Master."

We slapped hands on that.

"I needed to think, Punky," I said. "I've got to find a job that can make me five hundred dollars in two days. Otherwise, I can kiss Avery good-bye. Then I got to turn around and make six thousand dollars *before* school starts."

"Girl, shut up. Ain't nobody make that kind of money but drug dealers."

I shook my head in agreement. Who was I kidding? How many doctors did I know? None. How many doctors came out of this project? None. Doctors didn't even have offices near where we lived. I'd been fooling myself long enough. Swimming was all that was left. Maybe I could make it as a swimmer?

We walked on home, with Punky making mouth music all the way. Sometimes I wish I was his age. Didn't nothing really matter to me then. But I know that's a lie. Even when I was his age, things that hurt me mattered. For a fleeting second I thought about my daddy never coming 'round. That had been my pain when I was Punky's age. But never, never no more. I got bigger things to think about.

At home in bed I cried myself to sleep and dreamed of making a swimming commercial. But when I woke up—I woke up. How many swimming commercials with black people had I ever seen? That was easy—none.

The next morning Mama woke me up.

"Mama, why you ain't at work?" I asked her.

"You know the drill. Not enough people coming in. Too many hands, not enough mops. I got laid off. But now you tell me, what is this?"

Dang, I'd left the stupid letter on the nightstand. She had a hand on her hip and the other hand to hold the letter . . . I knew the look. I was in trouble. "It's a letter from Avery," I said, hoping that was the end of the conversation.

"And you didn't bother to show it to me? It says you have an appointment Thursday morning and you're supposed to bring your parents. So what were you planning?"

"Mama, if you read it, then you also know it says I need to bring a five hundred dollar deposit. I don't have the money. My plan is not to go."

"So you gon' give up just like that? Girl, you crazy. You don' spent an entire year bugging about how you going to *Avery*. Then you jump on a teacher 'cause she mess it up for you. But you got sense enough to call them and get the appointment yourself. And now you gon' just up and quit?"

"Mama, you know I don't have no five hundred dollars. I know you don't. Rhenda don't. Punky don't. So what you expect me to do?"

"How many times I gotta tell you kids you ain't living in my pocketbook. You don't know what I got. Any other time you ask me for whatever you want. Don't I get it for you?"

"Yes, ma'am," I said, wondering where this lecture was headed, because I knew she didn't have that kind of money.

"Well, for your information I'm taking you to the interview. And I'll have the money when you need it. So get up and get on out of here."

"But, Mama . . ." I began.

"Don't Mama me. That bus will be here any minute. You know they hate it when you late."

She walked out of the room. Rhenda was still asleep. Tomika was awake, playing with her teddy bear. It used to be mine until I was nine. Then all of a sudden I hated it. I can't remember why. I still never touch it now. I gave it to Punky when he was little, and now Tomika had it. I looked at her. I wondered what Tomika was going to be like when she grew up. I hope whatever happened she didn't fall back in the same old traps we seem to be tripping around in. I got dressed and caught the minibus.

I couldn't imagine where Mama could get the deposit money. Maids got laid off all the time, so they went from one low-paying motel to another to work. You almost had to have a college degree to work in the fancy hotels. Plus, Mama couldn't work where they'd report her money, so that left her with only a handful of sleaze-joints. Maybe she was out looking for another job? By the time I got to the center and rode over to the pool, I was trying to think about swimming. The only thing left for me.

I looked for Mr. Walt. Maybe talking to him might make me feel better, but he wasn't around yet.

Betty showed up after skipping yesterday. I asked her, "Where were you?"

She asked me, "You swimming or what?" and dived into the water.

"Hey, you okay?" I asked when I swam up near her.

"Yeah. Don't be buggin'. I come to swim with you."

"Okay," I said, accepting she didn't want to talk about whatever it was bothering her. We got in the same lane. I swam, and she followed me. We didn't ride the waves when coach was around, though. He wanted us swimming against each other, not with each other. The swim helped me a little. It forced Avery to the back of my mind.

We got out of the pool and sat on the bleachers.

Betty slammed her bag down and kicked her sneakers. Then she just sat picking at her nails, not talking or looking at me.

Finally, I said, "You coming over today?"

"Nope. I'm busy," she said.

"I'm probably going to hang home," I said.

"Ain't that just nothing. All of a sudden you gon' hang home, huh?"

"What are you talking about?" I asked her.

"I heard you been taking late night walks. Trying to get your groove on with dudes. You know what I'm saying?"

"What is wrong with you?" I said, my jaw tensing up. "Why you acting so crazy? And no. I don't know what you're saying."

"I'm outta here," she said, slapping the towel on the floor as she headed for the dressing room.

"Wait a minute," I said, following her. "I want to know what you mean by what you just said."

"You know what I meant. Don't play dumb with me, Miss Brains. You think Jeebie ain't tell me you was trying to do the hookup with him."

"Now I *know* you crazy. Ain't nobody in their right mind want no Jeebie," I said. I felt furious that he'd lied and twisted what had happened the night before. The dog. "Don't trip, Betty. You know me better than that."

"You the one trippin'. And think on it. I thought you was my girl. Yeah. You wanting to be somebody's girl, all right, trying to act like he ain't good enough for me but he's all right for you, though," she said. "By the way, give me back my bracelet."

Tears burned my eyes. "Here," I said, barely able to get it off my wrist because my hands trembled so badly. "Take the damn bracelet. I don't need it. If you're stupid enough to believe anything that lying—"

"Hey, what is all this yelling about?" Mr. Walt said, walking up.

Betty snatched the bracelet from my hand and said, "Stay away from him," and then walked off.

I watched her toss the bracelet in the trash and disappear.

"Are you all right, Keisha?" Mr. Walt asked, coming closer. "What are you crying about? That Betty," he said, shaking his head. "That girl is nutty."

I didn't want to agree. I wanted to say, "No she isn't." But I couldn't. I walked over to the trash can and peered inside to make sure she'd actually ditched the bracelet. It was there. I hated that damn Jeebie. I thought about taking it out. But if she didn't want me to have it over that lowlife, I didn't want it.

"Take a few minutes and get yourself together," Mr. Walt said, patting me on the back. "Don't worry about it."

A few minutes later I heard Mr. Walt shouting and blowing his whistle. "Let's go. Time to hit the water. Everybody. You too, Keisha."

I stood up.

After practice, Clarissa and Phyllis walked over
to me, both wearing smiles on their faces. Clarissa said,
"Would you like to come with us today? To my house?"

"For what?"

"We could all go to the movies and then just come
back and swim or something," she said.

"You have a pool at your house?" I asked her.

"Sure. What do you say?" Clarissa said, smiling. "You
want to come?"

No wonder she could swim. We had become sort of
friends since she'd taken up for me to get on the swim
team. I ain't saying I forgave her for liking Malik. But hey,

he liked her, too. As Grandma used to say, "Ain't no use fighting the truth 'bout something."

Phyllis stood silently, watching me like a cat.

"Why? Why do you want me to come over?" I asked.

Clarissa smiled. "I like you."

Phyllis said, "Me too. You're funny."

Yeah, a real clown, I thought, remembering my mama saying white people don't mind black people entertaining them. "What is that supposed to mean?"

"It means you're fun to be with," Phyllis said. "You're witty, is more what I meant. Hey, why are you giving us the third degree? You've got a chip on your shoulder, you know that, Keisha? We thought maybe we could be friends or like big sisters to you. But I told Clarissa this would happen."

"Listen," Clarissa said. "Sure, at first we were a little snotty, I'll admit."

"I wasn't," Phyllis said, interrupting.

"Yes, you were," Clarissa said. "Probably even more than me. But that's not important. What's important is we're all friends now. And friends visit each other."

"Yeah," I said. "Then why don't you come to my house?" This would shut them up.

Clarissa smiled. "Have you ever invited me? Or Phyllis?"

"No," I said, biting my lower lip. "But even if I did, you wouldn't come."

"Why not? I go to Phyllis's all the time."

"Phyllis?" I said, laughing. "Are you for real? There is nothing that's the same between me and Phyllis, honey. Phyllis might be black in color, but—"

"Don't go there," Phyllis said.

I looked at her. "Don't go there?" I said, shocked that she knew the expression. "Don't go there?" I repeated.

"What is up with you?" Phyllis said. "I thought you were smart. Do you really think you're blacker than me?"

"You got that right," I said, my hands on my hips.

She put her hands on hers, too, and said, "You're just like the rest of them."

"Who *you* calling them?" I asked. *"Black people?"*

"No," she said, quickly, *"Ignorant people.* You don't get it, do you? I'm black and I know it. In fact, I like it. I've been to Africa, have you? I speak an African language, and it's not Swahili. Do you? One of my favorite singing groups is African. What about you? Who is your favorite? I'm just as black as you, and don't you forget it. See, I know what you don't seem to know. There is nothing that says black people can't be educated, savvy, and smart, and still be black. In fact, if you get right down to it, my skin might be lighter, but I'm blacker than you. I really don't have to defend that I'm black. I just am and I love it."

"Enough of this," Clarissa said. "Are you coming or not?"

What could I say but, "I have to call my mama first."

While I waited for Mama to come to the telephone, I thought about what Phyllis said. It made sense to me. What made me think of her as white? Did the fact that she had money make her white? Jeebie had some money, and I never thought of him as white. Me, I was smart, could speak excellent English when I wanted to—did that make me white? Was being smart just for white people? Heck, no. Mr. Hakim's words came back to me. So why was I trippin' all this time?

"Mama," I said, when she finally came to the phone, "what took you so long?"

"Nothing, I was just coming in the house, that's all."

"Where've you been? Did you get a job?"

"Been someplace taking care of my business, Keisha Wright," she said.

I could almost see her smiling. She was up to something. "Mamaaaaa," I said, "what is it?"

"What is what?" she said. "I know you ain't call here to be asking me where I been. What do you want?"

"You're not going to tell me where you been?"

"Nope. And I'm gonna hang up if you don't hurry. I'm busy, Keisha," she said, chuckling. "You think I ain't got nothing better to do than mess with you all day?"

Huh-huh. She was up to something, all right. "Mama, can I go home with Clarissa? You know the counselor who drives the van to take me swimming. Phyllis, the other counselor, is going, too. They said they'd bring me home."

"Yeah. Where they live?" Mama said. "Are their parents home? Let me speak to her."

"Here we go," I said, sighing. "Clarissa, my mama wants to interrogate you," I said, handing her the receiver.

Clarissa said she lived in Fountainhead. Her mother was home. "Sure, Ms. Wright. I'll get Keisha back by nine," she said before hanging the telephone up.

"She asks way too many questions," I said, gathering up my stuff. "Let's go, before she calls back."

We had a great time.

We went to see a movie. It was Phyllis's pick and to my surprise it was a movie starring rappers. Clarissa had more rap CDs than I'd ever seen in my life. I forgot about my problems and just tried to enjoy the time. Clarissa even had a room she called her studio, where she did art stuff, like sculptures. She had plaster and crap everywhere.

Phyllis told me she was going to attend her mother's alma mater, Spelman, in Atlanta. Go figure. I would have never pegged her for someone who knew where Spelman was.

I had a lot to learn about living, that was sure. By the time I got home it was almost dark. I was glad, actually. After being in Clarissa's mansion I felt awkward when she pulled up to our tiny, junky-looking place. I couldn't recall feeling like this before. This was a different feeling than when Mr. Walt drove me home. This was like almost ashamed. Maybe I was ashamed.

"Hey," Clarissa called to me when I stepped out of the car. "When are you inviting *us* over?"

I turned around. Was she making fun of me? I could see it in her face, though—she was serious.

"Yeah," Phyllis said, "I want to meet your sister. She's our age, right?"

"And I've got to see her baby," Clarissa added. "I love babies."

"I don't know," I stammered, unprepared to deal with

this. "Plus, Tomika is not a baby. She's two years old. Of course, Rhenda acts like she's one."

"Well, it better be soon. We only have a few weeks in the program, and then we both head for college."

"Okay," I said, and waved good-bye as they pulled off. Who was I kidding? I *was* ashamed for them to come in my house. House? I had always referred to our three-bedroom government cookie-cutter apartment as "our house." But today I'd been in a real house with a screened-in porch, a maid, and a swimming pool, and even a little cabana, as Clarissa called it, for you to change clothes in. How could I call where I lived a "house" ever again?

My mind hurt when I went to bed.

"What's wrong with you?" Rhenda said.

"Nothing."

"Don't even try it. What is it?"

"Rhenda," I said, realizing it was useless to try hiding anything from her. She was like a radar machine when it came to me. Ever since we were little she was always prying my every thought out of me. She'd wanted to be a psychiatrist when she was younger. I thought about that. Younger. God, she was only seventeen now. But she seemed old to me. "Have you ever been ashamed of where we live?"

"Nope," she said, tickling Tomika. The baby had on frilly pink pajamas with white rabbits all over. Rhenda bought her too many clothes.

"Oh," I said, feeling even worse about my own feelings.

"Okay. Maybe. Why?"

I told her about what happened. About how I'd felt at Clarissa's, and then how I'd prayed they didn't come in when we got back to our apartment.

"I felt that way before," she said.

"I thought you said nope."

"I lied. Hey, when you go out and see all that stuff, it can make you shame. I know. Don't feel bad. Just forget about it. Don't go over there no more."

"I don't think that'll help. When did you feel like it, anyway? You never told me. I thought we told each other everything?"

"Girl, you ain't old enough to know everything about my business."

"Really, you forget you told me when you . . . you know, did it the first time."

"Yeah, and I shouldn't have—you know, did it. That's why I told you. Look. This is who we are. We poor black people, and that's that."

I heard it for the first time, her calling us poor. And something else in her voice I'd never heard before, or at least never paid attention to. Something that wasn't there when she was my age and always telling me about the car she was going to have, and the house with the maid and stuff. Actually, it wasn't so much what was there but what wasn't there. "Rhenda. Can I ask you something personal?"

"Like more personal than when you ask me every month did my period come on?" she said, laughing.

"Yeah. More personal than that." I smiled. "You so

silly. Anyway, why you never tell me Mama used to be smart in school?"

"I don't know," she said, now staring at Tomika.

I could tell she was purposely not looking at me. "I know you, Rhenda. You know why you do things. Why you never tell me? Do you remember Mama telling you?"

"Why? She tell *you?*" she asked, sighing. Still focused on Tomika.

"No, Mr. Walt said it when he first was over here. Then when I asked Mama why she never tell me, she said it's because when she told you it hurt you some kind of way."

"Mama said that?"

"Well, not in so many words. But I knew what she meant. I told her that didn't make sense."

"Hmm. Mama is truly smart, then," Rhenda said, making the kind of laugh you make to keep your heartbreak from showing.

"Tell me. How could knowing that hurt you? I *like* knowing she was smart in school."

"I ain't never told nobody this. And you better not tell Mama."

"I won't. I promise." I knew this was serious. Mama warned us as little girls not to learn to keep secrets from one another. She said that's how men can molest children by telling them something should be a secret from their mamas. She said, "Never keep secrets from your mama. Know that you can tell your mama anything and she gon' do something about it. Your mama is God's weapon on the earth, sent here to protect you."

So it wasn't often me and Rhenda kept a secret from Mama. And God forbid Mama ever find out. "I cross my heart," I reassured her.

"I been thinking about this a lot lately. When Mama told me she was an A student in school—I don't know if I realized what it did inside of my mind. You know it seemed okay at the time she told me. But later, when I started looking around and thinking about it, I suppose it didn't mean the same to me no more."

"What do you mean?"

"See, I started thinking, at least I think this is what my mind started thinking, if Mama was smart and she had a good mama and a real house, 'cause you know when Grandma lived and Mama and her brothers and sisters lived over in Walkertown in a house, what Mama calls their old home place, you know in a house they owned, with a good neighborhood . . . and Grandma worked for some white people cooking but she took good care of her children . . .

"So I started thinking then, that if Mama couldn't get out of high school, no matter how smart she was, no matter she makes good grades, then maybe it ain't no way to escape. You know, 'cause she strong, smart, and all and she still couldn't do it. I started comparing the way Grandma used to be able to buy Mama stuff and then she died and Mama and them lost their house and then Mama had me and she had to go on welfare and stuff and she still trying, but nothing work for her."

"Rhenda. What are you talking about? First off, Mama buy us stuff, too. And if that's what you were thinking that Mama could have finished school if she hadn't had you—then why you go and have a baby? That doesn't make sense."

"You're right. Now—it doesn't make sense to me, either. But back then, when I was fourteen, everybody in school was acting like 'cause you black, school ain't no way out—not for real. You know some of my teachers, especially the white ones, would say to me, 'Rhenda, you ought to go to cosmetology school when you graduate. You can fix hair so good'? Never, 'We believe you can become a psychiatrist.' Go to medical school or whatever. And then Mama, she was always warning me to stay away from boys or I was gonna get pregnant like she did, and—"

I frowned. "And so—you did? What sense does that make, Rhenda?"

"None. But when it was happening, I don't know, maybe I wasn't as smart as you. I don't know. I just know I started thinking stuff, like my being able to go to college ain't gonna work. I'm going to end up stuck here forever and I might as well face it. Some black people get out, but most of them don't.

"Then I met Michael, and he was all 'I love you, baby.' And, 'We can get married and buy a house.' And I was thinking, Shit, if I got a man who gonna take care of me, what do I need to finish school for? I can get married and have a job making twice the money Mama's making. I felt like Michael was the only man who ever really loved me. We was going to get married and live happily ever after.

"Then he told me he didn't want no kids till later. But I heard he'd been going out with another girl, so I figure

I'm gonna lose my big chance for a good husband and a house so I got pregnant. And believe me, it wasn't ever like I was thinking I'm gonna trap him or nothing. It just happened."

Rhenda was crying now. Holding Tomika up to her face and crying almost the way she does when she's tickling Tomika, blowing into her stomach.

I wanted to cry, too. Because it still made no sense to me at all. And now I could see it didn't make sense to Rhenda, but it was too late. It didn't matter. Just 'cause something don't make sense don't mean it won't happen.

"You know what is the worse part?" she asked me in between sobs.

I shook my head.

"That I absolutely *hate* Michael now. I can't even see what I liked about him. He's selfish and pigheaded, and his feet stink."

I laughed through my tears. "His feet stink?"

"Yeah. When I moved over there in his mama's apartment when I was pregnant, I realized I didn't even want no house with a stinky feet man that wouldn't even clean up his own room. Or, a man that yelled at his own mother.

"That's when I came home. I said, let me get my sorry ass back home with my family. Michael's family crazy.

"That's something Mama kept saying to me. She kept telling me you gotta marry somebody who has the same values you do. But I wish she'd just said something like, you gotta make sure you marry a man whose whole family ain't nuts, or you gotta marry a man who knows that

141

buying your baby a pair of Nikes ain't taking care of it, or even more important, you gotta marry somebody that knows to take a bath every day and change your socks if you don't want your feet to stink."

By now we were both laughing. Rhenda said, "It ain't no fun getting pregnant and having no baby. Don't get me wrong. I love Tomika, but I sure wish now I'd listened to Mama. I don't want you to make the same mistake. That's why I'm glad you ain't boy crazy like I was."

I didn't answer her; I just got up and went to the bathroom. All that laughing was about to make me pee on myself. Plus, I needed sleep.

The next day, Wednesday, Coach worked us hard at practice. First we did stretching exercises, which I absolutely hate. If I've got to exercise I want to get it over with—fast. I don't want no warming-up mess. Then we ran around the building six times, which always makes my knees feel like they're cracking open. Then there's the jump roping, which puzzles me that I could have ever thought double Dutching was fun. Finally we swam for a while. We could hear Coach yelling on the sidelines, "Come on, let's swim, Keisha. You, too, Betty. Okay, take a deep breath. Hit the water, lift your head, suck in air."

Betty left at the break, after ignoring me all morning. I lay down on the bench and fell asleep, dreaming of me telling Betty about how we fish. I was saying to her what I always said when we raced: "Betty, me and you, we fish. Can't nobody stop us from swimming. Can't nobody stop us from winning—you know why—we fish." I must have been out of it. The next thing I knew, the whistle sounded and I saw Coach standing at the side of the pool. We had started calling him the Terminator. And for good reason.

I got home tired and wiped out. We'd swam about a million laps. Swim to the wall, flip over, swim back. Over and over. I wouldn't be surprised if I wasn't growing fins by now.

Punky lay on the living room floor watching TV with his legs crossed at the knee and his arms under his head. "Thanks for helping me out the other night, Punky," I said when I walked in. "You could've gotten hurt, though, boy. I thought for a second I was gonna have to jump you."

"Yeah. You know better. Girl, you better quit sneaking out, though. I ain't gonna be around to watch your back forever."

"Where you gon' be," I said, hitting him playfully on the head.

"Hey, it's you who ain't gon' be here. I heard you was going to college after all. I hope you smoke 'em."

"Thanks, I hope so, too," I said. "Punky, where's Mama?"

"In the kitchen."

"And Rhenda?"

"Hey, why can't you walk in there and see where they at? I'm busy, now how's about that."

I lowered my voice. "I got to ask you something."

"What?" he said, still looking at the television screen.

I knelt down and whispered into his ear, "Do you know where Mama is getting the money for the college deposit?"

Punky was only a kid, but he knew a lot of people in the

neighborhood. He was small for his size, and for some reason, people didn't always notice him. He could find out almost anything. He claimed he was going to be a spy when he got older. Rhenda said if he didn't quit hanging out so much, he was gonna be a dead spy, since Mama was gonna kill him. He was a good kid. Nosy, though. Right now I was hoping he'd live up to his reputation.

"I don't know," he said, looking up for the first time. "You know, Mama. She don't tell nobody her business."

"Do you know if she was out today?"

"Nope. And you better forget it, 'cause if she find out you snooping in her business, she gon' bust you. And you better let her know I ain't asking 'bout it with you, 'cause my name is Les and I ain't in this mess."

"Okay. Okay," I said, knowing he was right.

Rhenda walked in, holding Tomika in her arms. She said, "Hey. Mama want you in the kitchen."

"Okay. But Rhenda, you gon' spoil that baby. Why don't you let her walk sometime? She's too old for you to hold all the time."

Punky said, "I don' told her. The baby gon' forget *how* to walk."

"'Cause I don't want to, that's why. She my baby, and if I want to carry her, I can. You two better mind your own business."

"Okay. Okay," I said.

In the kitchen, Mama sat at the red ceramic-topped table. It had a burn mark where Rhenda had left a hot plate on it once when the stove broke down.

"Sit down," she said. "I've got to talk to you."

This was serious. I could see the lines in her forehead. "Ma'am?"

"Tomorrow, when we go to the interview, I want you to remember something. I want you to know that people make their own bed to lie in. Me, I made mine and I have to lie in it. Rhenda, she don' made hers. You still got time to make yours up better. I want that for you. Now, go look in your room."

On the bed was a navy blue suit and white blouse, and pair of navy blue pumps sat beside them. "Mama," I whispered to myself, torn between being happy and scared where the money came from. This wasn't no Kmart or Target suit; this tag said PARISIANS. I know Mama. She ain't bought it hot, 'cause she hate stealing. And I also knew it was pointless asking her where the money came from, so I tried on the suit.

"Well, what you thinking?" Mama asked me, smiling, walking into the room. "I surprised you, didn't I? Where you think I been the other day when you on the phone trying to get in my business, girl? Your mama don't mess around. She straight up with what she gotta do."

"I love it, Mama. It's so, so . . ." I said, whirling around in the floor.

"Sophisticated," she said. "I want you to have more'n I had, Keisha. You smart and you ain't got your mind stuck on boys like I did. If a person is truly smart, they'll make smart choices."

I sure didn't want her to get started on that, so I said quickly, "But Mama. Where did you get the money?"

"Noney. Now don't go dipping."

"I'm sorry. I just don't want to make things bad for all

of us. I've been thinking. I could get a job. You know, drop out of the at-risk thing. There's still a few weeks left in the summer. That way, I can save all my money for Avery. I probably won't have the whole six thousand dollars but maybe they'd do like payments or something. I didn't ask them about that."

"What about swimming, girl? You can't just drop out. You s'pose to be going to the Olympics in two years."

"Mama, swimming is fun. But it ain't going to get me into Avery."

"You leave Avery to me. I'm the mama here. Y'all going have to learn how to tend to your own business. That's your problem, you too grown," she said, leaving the room, mumbling.

I was glad. I hated the "too grown lecture" big time. I pranced around the house modeling my outfit until Punky said I was about to get on his last nerve walking in front of the television.

I went to bed early so I'd be ready.

The next morning when me and Mama left we were looking like we'd just stepped off the pages of *Essence* magazine. Mama had on her church clothes, and me, I had on my navy suit.

The interview was sort of touch-and-go. Three people all asking me questions at once. Why-do-you-want-to-come-to-Avery type questions. Questions I don' already answered on the paper. I thought it was going badly until they got up and said, "Welcome to Avery."

I just grinned. Then they turned me over to a financial officer named Ms. Ross. She was very small, with a tiny voice that put me in mind of chipmunks. Mama was in there with me.

"I'm so glad you can attend the fall session. We'll arrange with your school for you to come two hours twice a week. You can pay the deposit now. The balance is due on the fifteenth of October."

"Excuse me," I said, "but is there a payment plan for the balance?"

Mama shot me a dagger. "It's no problem. I'll have the money by then."

Miss Ross said, "We've never had a payment plan, but—"

"That's good," Mama said. "We don't need one."

When we left out I said, "Mama. Why did you tell her that?"

"I'll have the money. Now drop it," she said, clinching her teeth together, "or you won't go. And it won't be because of money."

But I knew there was as much chance of me going to Avery as being invited to the rap group Outkast's party. Unless I got a job or sold drugs, I could kiss Avery goodbye. It's funny how that thought crept into my mind. Selling drugs. What would be wrong with that? It ain't like I was forcing nobody to buy them.

I was distracted at swimming thinking about the drug thing. It was funny how you could rationalize almost anything when you needed to. By the time I went home I'd decided it wouldn't do for me. I ain't selling no drugs. That's like a free get-in-jail card.

I read for a time. When I went to bed, Mama still wasn't home.

In a while, Rhenda shook me. "You 'sleep?"

"No, not really," I said, turning over to look at her.

"Mama ain't gonna have that money, girl. I don't know why she trippin' but we both know she just being proud. But like Grandma say, 'Pride don't pay no bills.' I been thinking though, if I give you half of my welfare check, it might help some."

"Yeah," I said, sitting up, pretending to act excited. "And I could get a job like maybe, like, as a model, and then, like, I could be in movies and make millions of dollars and then I'd, like, have enough to pay like my money to like Avery."

"Oh, shut up. I'm serious," she said.

"I know you are," I said, smiling now. "But Rhenda, you could add up all your whole welfare check for six months, plus me working at Burger King, and I still wouldn't have that much money."

"You ain't never lied," she said.

We both burst into hysterical laughter.

Friday went fast. I practiced. Mama was in bed when I got home. Rhenda said, she'd been 'sleep most of the day. "Does she have a job?" I asked Rhenda.

"She won't say. You know Mama. Hey, maybe she's just tired and trying to catch up. Everybody need a break."

"You got that right. I need one now," I said, climbing into bed and falling sound asleep.

Saturday morning Betty called. "Jeebie said for
me to call you. I told him about what happened. He said
ain't no call for me to break up our friendship over him.
He said, What woman don't want him. So we cool. He
don't like his women feuding. You want to go out with
me and Jeebie and one of his friends?" she asked.

"Girl. You know my mama would kill me if she even
knew you were saying Jeebie's name over her telephone,"
I said, wondering if she'd lost her mind for real. "First
off," I continued, "I ain't feuding over Jeebie. He lying. I
ain't say nothing to him. You can ask Punky. He was right
there. And I wouldn't be caught dead with Jeebie."

"Oh, you too good to go out with me now?"

"Not you, Betty. Jeebie. In fact, you too good to go out with Jeebie."

"I don't wanna hear this shit," she said. "I told him you was gon' be buggin'. I thought you was my best friend. That is, until you turned into some damn white girl. Let me tell you something in case you don' forgot it. You black and you ain't gonna never be white, just like me. Try to remember that for me. Okay?"

She hung up.

I felt sick on the stomach. I couldn't think about it. I needed to mop the kitchen and take out the trash. Clarissa and Phyllis were stopping by.

Yesterday they said, "We're coming by your place tomorrow."

What was I going to say? No?

When I mentioned the possibility to Mama earlier she had said, "What are you worried about? If they're your friends, why wouldn't they stop by?"

Sometimes I wondered why she was never ashamed of where we lived or what we had. She acted like we might be living in Trump Tower somewhere and our maids were just on vacation.

Rhenda dressed Tomika up in a yellow sunsuit that had Popsicles all over it. She made some grape Kool-Aid for the "company."

I said, "I don't think rich people drink Kool-Aid."

She said, "Don't be stupid."

There was a knock on the door.

I brushed my hair quickly and threw the brush back in

my room. I heard it hit the floor as I opened the door and saw the kids on the stoop staring at Clarissa and Phyllis like they might have just landed from Mars. It occurred to me again how seldom I'd seen any white people in this neighborhood other than the police.

"Come on in," I said. "Have a seat." They were dressed in all white. They were going to play tennis afterward.

Rhenda had put a cloth on the sofa to hide the torn part.

It wasn't long before we were all laughing together.

Rhenda imitated Max from the television sitcom *Living Single* and we all cracked up.

The whole time, Clarissa held the baby. In fact, she wouldn't let anyone else hold the baby.

When Mama came in, I introduced her. She sat down and asked them a few questions like, Where did they plan on going to college? Then she looked at me and said, "Keisha, did you offer your friends something to drink?"

I dreaded the moment. "I don't think they want anything, Mama."

"Sure, we'll take something, thank you," Phyllis said, smiling.

I sat still. I hated to bring the Kool-Aid out. "But we don't have any sodas," I said.

"That's okay. I don't drink sodas," Clarissa said.

"What about Kool-Aid?" Phyllis asked. "Do you have any Kool-Aid? That's our favorite drink in the summer at my house."

"It is?" I said, like she might have just admitted they

lived on a spaceship and drank Tang-flavored cow manure for breakfast.

She looked at me strange. "What? You don't like Kool-Aid?"

"Sure we do," Rhenda said, grinning at me as if she'd won the lottery. "We've got grape with lemons in it."

"My all-time favorite," Phyllis said. "My mama still freezes ice pops for me. I know that sounds childish, but I love them just the same. She keeps teasing me about how difficult it's going to be to send me freeze pops through the mail to college."

Mama said, "Y'all want to see some pictures of Tomika when she was little?"

Clarissa said, "Yes," before anyone else could speak. She held Tomika on her lap while Mama told her about each photo.

Rhenda came back with a pitcher and four glasses. Mama started telling Clarissa a funny Tomika story.

We were all laughing when the taps came on the screen door.

Mama went to open it.

Betty stepped in. "Hi, Ms. Wright," she said, putting her hands on her hips and glaring over at me like I was the only snake in the room and my fangs were showing.

Mama said, "Hello," back. Then, "I'm going to take a bath. You girls have fun."

Rhenda got up and followed Mama out. I knew without telling her she would get Betty a glass for Kool-Aid, too. Rhenda was thoughtful like that.

Betty stood in the doorway until Mama and Rhenda left the room. Normally she would have plopped right down in a chair.

I said, "Come on in, Betty. Why you standing in the door like that?"

"I told Jeebie I couldn't go with him today. That I needed to spend some time with my best friend. He got mad but you know what? I didn't care."

"That's great," I said. Something wasn't right. Normally she'd have grabbed up Tomika and showered her with kisses before saying anything. "So why you looking at me like that? Sit your butt down," I said, wondering what the look meant.

"Now I see why you couldn't go, girlfriend. You were busy with your own best frieeeeends." She deliberately dragged the word out.

Clarissa shifted the baby in her arms.

Phyllis stopped flipping through the photo album and looked up.

"What are you talking about?" I asked, sensing a spark in the air that might explode any second.

"You. I'm talking about you, girlfriend. You think you're so damn special. You think you—"

Mama appeared at the hall door. "I know you ain't come up in my house cursing, Betty Shabazz."

"No, ma'am," she said, "I'm just leaving." Then she looked dead at me and said, "You ain't nothing to them but charity. You'll see 'fore it's over." Then she stormed out, slamming the screen door so hard, it vibrated.

Mama said, "Is that girl crazy?"

I didn't say anything. I was too hurt. Stunned. Betty was the first best friend I'd ever had besides Rhenda. I couldn't really say that about Clarissa or Phyllis. First off, they were older than me, and next year neither one of them would be around. And second they treated me like a little sister, really, not like their "best friend."

Rhenda had come in the room and caught the tail end of Betty's speech. "Don't worry about that, girl. She's just jealous."

"We're sorry," Clarissa said. "Would you like us to leave?"

I shook my head no. But I really did want them to leave—disappear. I wanted to run after Betty. But I didn't.

"Maybe it's for the best," Rhenda said later.

But how could losing Betty possibly be for the best?

Monday morning at the center I wished I had agreed with Rhenda.

"Hey, white girl," Betty said, standing with two other black girls and staring me down.

I ignored her and pulled out my gym bag to go to the pool.

When it was time to leave, she came over. "You can't piss on me no more. I'm quitting."

I looked at her. "What?"

"You heard me. I'm bustin' out of this joint. I got better things to do?"

"Look, if you're mad at me, that don't mean you have to quit. I won't bother you."

"That's the way it is with white folks, ain't it? They

154

think every thing in the universe got something to do with them. What's that? You so vain. I bet you think this song is about you."

"Betty, don't trip. I didn't mean it like that. I just thought—"

"I know what you thought."

"You're wrong about Clarissa. All white people ain't the same. She's really down with helping. She's the reason I got on the swim team—and you, too, for that matter. What about us going to the Olympics?"

"Yeah. So you cool with her and my brother, then?"

My skin crawled. "What is that supposed to mean?"

"It ain't mean nothing. She *your* friend. All I know is they do spend time together. I ain't saying they dating or nothing, but . . . since you don't care and that's *your* friend, I'm done. Anyway I've got things to do. Places to go."

"What are you talking about? What do you have to do that's so important you gon' lose your spot on the team? What about the big meet coming up? The Olympics guy who's coming to check us out. You just gonna blow all that? You can't, Betty."

"Oh, yeah I can. You'll see."

"What? Did you get a job? Tell me you ain't quitting school?" I said, reaching out to touch her arm.

She jerked away. "Don't touch me. I'm too delicate. And, hell yes, I quit. I ain't going to school and I ain't gon' have to work. I'm going be livin' large."

I bit my lip. What did she mean? "Betty," I said, "you better be careful. I don't know what you're talking about, but it don't sound like you know what you're doing."

"I know what I'm doing. I know, see," she said, tapping her stomach. "I'm having his baby."

"Whose baby?" I said, clinching my teeth so hard, my jaw hurt.

"Who you think?"

I wanted to hit her. Slam her against the locker. Knock some sense in her head. But I couldn't do nothing. I couldn't even answer her. A baby? She could barely take care of herself, and now she's talking about a baby. *Are we all crazy?*

I took her hand. She didn't jerk away. I could see tears in her eyes.

"You ain't pregnant by no Jeebie. I know you ain't. He's crazy. Don't you know he shot that girl," I said, snapping the fingers of my right hand and still holding on to her with my left. "What's her name?" I said, trying to remember.

"Sandra. Her name is Sandra. And Jeebie said she tried to take him to court for child support when he was already paying her money."

"You believe that?" I asked. "You know he lying. Everybody know he shot that girl 'cause she got pregnant again and she wouldn't get no abortion. What? You think there's a reason somebody should be able to shoot you five times?"

I stood there hating Jeebie more than any person I ever hated in my life—even my daddy. I said, "Jeebie is a low-down-dirty-drug-dealing-dog who don't care 'bout nobody. Hell, that man curse his own mama out." I wanted to hate Betty for being so damn ignorant. I cried.

She started crying, too, 'cause, even if she don't say it, she know she being stupid.

As we hugged each other I thought, If all the tears cried in poor neighborhoods ran together, we'd be swimming in the ocean. Shakespeare must have known more black people than Othello when he was writing them tragedies.

She finally pulled away and said, "The hell with the Olympics. I got my own plans," and walked out.

I didn't see Betty on Tuesday, and by Friday she'd missed every practice. Finally, I asked Malik when I saw him without Clarissa stuck in his face, "Where's your sister?"

He looked at me funny. Like I'd said something stupid.

"She's at your house, ain't she?" he answered. "She called me and said your mama said she could stay there until she felt better."

"Today? Betty called you today? She's at our apartment now?"

"No. Not today. She called me Sunday night and said she was hanging with you for a few days until she was better. She said, you know"—he held his head down, obviously embarrassed—"she said she was on the rag and didn't want to be fighting with nobody at our house."

I was shaking my head. "I'm calling Mama." I ran to the pay phone in the hall and fished inside my change purse that I have pinned to my towel for a quarter. Then I remembered it was thirty-five cents.

Malik had followed me and he handed me a dime.

I dropped the money in the slot and punched in our number. The phone rang six times. Finally Mama answered, sounding like she had marbles in her mouth. "Are you 'sleep, Mama?" I asked her, wondering why she'd be asleep this time of day. She told me she didn't get a job. But now wasn't the time to ask. "Mama, have you seen or talked to Betty?"

"I ain't talked to her, not since she came over here last week, but I seen her."

"Where you seen her?"

"You heard about it. God, I didn't want you to hear on no street."

"Heard what, Mama? Where did you see her? Coming out of their apartment? At our apartment?"

"What she saying?" Malik asked, trying to snatch the phone.

"Wait," I said to him. "Mama where did you see her?" I thought, Oh my God, maybe she lost her baby. I knew she wouldn't get an abortion. She didn't believe in abortions. She loved babies. The first time she was at my house, I recalled how she said she wanted a baby like Rhenda. She could have had a miscarriage or something.

"You haven't heard, then?" Mama said, sighing heavily.

"Heard what, Mama? Please quit stalling!"

"She was at the Grand. I stopped by to get my last paycheck and I seen her when they brought her out on the stretcher and put her in the ambulance."

"Oh, no. No!" I screeched. I could barely hold the phone to my ear. All the muscles went dead in my hand.

"Somebody hurt her up bad," Mama said. "She's at Brady Hospital."

I dropped the phone down. It clattered bang, bang, bang, against the wall. I slid to the floor.

Malik picked up the receiver and I heard him asking Mama what was wrong with me? When he got off the phone, he scooped me up under the arms until I was standing. "Come on. We got to get to the hospital quick."

I was crying as he pulled me along.

"We gon' get a taxi," he said. "That'll be faster. I got some money."

As we rushed to the door of the center, Clarissa ran up. "What's the matter? Where are you going?"

Malik stopped for a second, looked at her, shrugged, and then turned and pulled me out the door. Clarissa followed, trotting alongside, asking him questions. I heard her but I didn't care about what she was saying. I only cared about Betty.

When Malik whistled for the first taxi that passed, it slowed, the driver looked out at him, and speeded away. It was getting dark. The chances of Malik hailing a taxi in his gym shorts and no shirt and me in my bathing suit with a towel draped around my shoulders were zero. I was still barefooted. Malik had on sandals, but everybody knows even if he'd had on an expensive suit, the taxis would have kept zooming by—leastways, everybody black knows.

Clarissa said, "Come on, I'll take you in my van."

I hated that she had the transportation and we didn't. A thought settled in my mind, before it went blank: Without a white girl we couldn't even get to the hospital. It was funny to me that under stress I still thought of Clarissa as a white girl. Not my friend first. But a rich white girl.

At the hospital only Malik was allowed to go with the doctor to see Betty.

I paced back and forth in the waiting area, wringing the end of my towel and crying.

Clarissa questioned the nurses like she was in charge. And for some reason the black nurse answered her.

She finally came over to me and said, "Somebody beat her up and shot her in the stomach. She was pregnant and lost the baby. She's in critical condition, Keisha. They won't know until the morning whether she'll make it. Only her close family can see her. Is there anyone I should call? Do they have a telephone?"

Do they have a telephone? I wanted to shout, Why are you even here? She's not your best friend. She doesn't even like you. In fact, she hates all white people. But instead I moved away from Clarissa and called Mama collect. She was coming and bringing anyone from Malik's house who wanted to come with her. "Hold tight," is what she said.

So I sat down and held myself tight like my grandma taught me to do when I was a little girl and I believed in the boogeyman. My grandma would say, "Baby girl, there ain't no such thing as a boogeyman. There is only one person who can save you from evil, baby, and that's you. Ain't no evil out there that's bigger than God." But obviously Grandma didn't know people like Jeebie. I know he is the one who shot Betty. And if I could see him now, I'd kill him myself.

When Mama came, Malik was still not back. She brought Betty's mama and stepdaddy. According to Betty, they had changed their names to Shabazz many years before. I decided, as I watched them now, that it had happened long before drugs and alcohol knew them. I'd never seen Betty's mother close up. She probably had been a pretty lady. I thought, That's where Malik gets his looks.

Betty and Malik's mama's arms were scarred from needles. She was so thin, I thought she'd break if she walked into something too hard. Her hair was sprawled all over her head and sticking up in places. When she sat down, I could see she didn't have on stockings or socks. Her sneakers were gray, but you could tell they were supposed to be white.

Mama was neat and clean looking even though she had on her old-lady work shoes. I loved my mama.

Malik's stepdaddy and his mama were crying now, his mama wiping snot with bits of a dissolved tissue. The stepdaddy stood quietly, letting his tears run down his face.

Malik came out the double swinging doors with the

doctor and walked over to his mama. He sat in a chair beside her and took her scrawny hand into his hands. He started rubbing her hand and talking to her softly.

I thought about him rubbing Betty's forehead, and a shiver went through me. The way you feel when you ride over a steep hill real fast in a car. I couldn't believe I was thinking about how good he looked. Girls can be so sickening.

The stepdaddy stood alongside the chair, watching Malik.

Mama whispered to me, "That's Malik's stepdaddy. I know him from way back. He used to be a musician. Drinking stopped all that. I didn't want to tell you before. Now it doesn't matter. You can see why Betty was hanging out at our house."

I shook my head that I understood.

I glanced over at Clarissa. She was crying. Standing alone.

I wanted to go over to her and comfort her. But I felt confused inside. Why did I feel so hostile toward her, like somehow by being here to witness this she'd done something wrong? She hadn't. But for now, I just let her stand by herself, sniffling.

Finally, she walked over to Malik and said, "I'm sorry. If there's anything I can do, let me know. Don't worry, I'll cover for you."

Then she walked over to me and Mama. She touched my hand. "It'll be all right, Keisha. Call me later, okay?" And she left. I wondered what she would have to "cover" for Malik for, but then a doctor walked out.

He called Malik over and whispered something to him. Malik said a few words that I couldn't make out. Then he walked back and took his mama by the arm and helped her up.

He said, "Come on, Daddy. We gotta go in to see her. They think she ain't gonna make it." He coughed, choking back tears. "The doctor say she ain't fighting to stay alive no more."

I could see the pain breaking up Malik's face. Then he turned back to me and Mama and said, "Hey, ain't y'all coming? I told them you family too."

I followed them into the room with my mama holding me up so I wouldn't just fall down and start screaming like I knew she knew I wanted to.

Malik kneeled down beside the bed and kissed Betty. He started stroking her forehead. Just like before, at the beach.

Their mama began wailing, "My baby. Oh Lord, my baby. I don' killed my baby." And then she passed out.

Two nurses and an orderly carried her from the room. The doctor followed them.

Their stepdaddy was blabbering something about God saving his daughter and he'd stop drinking.

All I could feel was a big burning hole inside.

Malik motioned for me.

I sat on the side of the bed slowly so I wouldn't jar Betty. I lifted her hand. It felt soft and warm, not cold like I thought it would feel. She was hooked up to a lot of tubes like a scene from television. I whispered to her, "Betty. Betty can you hear me? I'm here with you, girl. I know you ain't still mad at me. You my best friend, ain't *nobody* change that."

I leaned over close to her face. She had a funny smell about her, like maybe she was willing death to rot her body. "You hear me, Betty. You remember how you almost drowned that time. And I told you later when you learned to swim how you was so brave. Betty, I know you brave now too. I want you to swim, Betty. Come on. Remember how we used to pull each other through the water. Riding the waves. And then we would be swimming side by side. Remember? We'd take turns swimming on the tail of each other's ripples in the water and that would make us both go faster. Remember? We said we could win any race together. Remember we said that? We were going to the Olympics, remember? You and me, the first black girl swimmers going to the Olympics. Remember?

"Come on, let's swim, Betty. Okay, take a deep breath. Hit the water, lift your head, suck in air, Betty. Come on, in, then out. In, then out. Can't you just hear Mr. Walt saying it now? Come on, Betty, kick your feet. Get going, get some speed. Keep your rhythm now. Swim, girl. Okay, move, glide, swim, fight the water, move through that water, cut it up, move so you can feel the burning in your chest."

I was gasping now. Tears flowing down my face like faucet water, sweat beading my upper lip, snot running out my nose. Guilt choked the life out of me. I thought, I love Betty and I have to make her come back. I have to.

I got down on my knees. My heart over her heart. My

breath, her breath. I whispered close to her ear, "Come on Betty. We like fish. Fish in the ocean. Remember. Fish swimming out from inside our mamas. We fighters, Betty. Remember I told you that. That's why we here. We fish swimming out so we can breathe. So we can live in this world, Betty. Good fish. Betty. They trying to catch us up in their hooks, Betty. But we fish that don't have to bite that hook. Remember I told you that. Me and you, we fish. Can't nobody stop us from swimming. Can't nobody stop us from winning, 'cause we fish." I said it, over and over, until I couldn't tell if my mouth was moving anymore. I didn't know if Malik was there. I didn't know if anyone was there but me and Betty. We were fish.

Then a beep went off, loud, shrill, insistent. I evidently had blanked out, because suddenly people were shoving me aside. A nurse pushed me outside the door.

I heard scrambling. Commotion. Noise. Beeps. Shouts. I was swimming. Swimming to my freedom. Struggling to stay alive. Me and Betty we had to fight to breathe. We weren't nothings. We were fish.

Suddenly Mama was whispering to me. I heard her. She was calling my name. "Keisha. Keisha, baby. Keisha. Come on now, snap out of it. Come on, baby. Mama is here."

When I opened my eyes I was sitting on my mama's lap out in the hallway, shivering from the coldness of the air-conditioning, and from shock. The lights were shining brightly, making me squint. My mama cradled me in her arms. She was sitting in the rocker that had been in Betty's room. She rocked me back and forth, rubbing my forehead in long, slow strokes. She had draped her own sweater over me.

My mama whispered, "She's okay, baby. Whatever you were doing must have made her fight harder. They say her heart started pumping real fast and the doctors needed to help her better or something, but they say she's got a fifty-fifty chance now."

Malik was sitting on the hall floor, crying into his hands.

I wanted to get up and say something, but I couldn't. I was tired and foggy-feeling.

Finally he walked over and knelt down in front of me. "You aw-right?"

"Yeah," I said, even though I felt like I imagined how being drunk must feel.

"Good," Malik said, looking down at his feet while he balanced himself in a squat. He wiped his eyes and said, "Thanks. Okay. Thanks for helping my sister out." Then he stood up and walked down the hall and disappeared into a room.

Mama said, "They had to sedate his mama. She's in that room. You did a good thing for your friend, baby."

"Thanks, Mama," I said, gasping with tears. "I love Betty, Mama."

"I know. I know. Now let's go get something hot for you to drink. And then we'll go home. You can come back tomorrow. I got to go get some sleep. I work in a few hours."

I hugged her and she hugged me back. We got up and walked down the hall arm in arm.

I hated later that I'd not been paying attention to what Mama said that day. "I work in a few hours." I figured she must have gotten a new maid's job after all, but I wished I'd just asked her. Somehow it flew over my head like an unnoticed bird.

It was a few days after Betty got hurt that I thought about it. I was at swim practice when the words sort of just came to me. Another girl had replaced Betty on the swim team, but she was nowhere near as fast.

No arrest had been made in Betty's shooting, but we all knew who did it. I hated that whoever saw it wouldn't come forward. Sometimes people were just too scared to tell on drug dealers. Scared they gon' come after them next.

But the word on the street was that Malik told Jeebie if he ever came near his sister again or laid a hand on anyone in his family, he'd be wearing slugs as body organs. In other words, he'd be dead.

When I got home from the center, Punky was sitting in the corner of his room, crying. I walked over and slid down beside him, hugging my knees. "What's wrong with you, boy?" He normally didn't cry unless he got mad.

"Nothin'," he said between sniffles.

"Then why you in here crying for nothin'?" I laid my hand on his arm.

He pulled it away. "Leave me alone."

"What's the matter?" I said. "Where's Rhenda?" She handled him better than I did when he was upset.

Punky shrugged.

I tried to recall whether she had an appointment with welfare for something. One thing welfare is good for is setting appointments to pry in your business. But Rhenda wouldn't leave home unless she knew Punky wouldn't be alone. "Where's Mama, then? Ain't she home?"

"Mama?" He looked at me like I'd slapped him. "Mama ain't *been* home."

"What do you mean?" I said, my heart beating faster.

"She ain't come home last night," he said.

"You *crazy*. She was in her bed when I left this morning."

"Yeah. Did you see her?"

He had me there. I hadn't seen her since yesterday

evening at supper. She'd said she had a migraine and was going to bed. She said for us not to bother her. When she had a migraine we didn't bother her because she would snap your head off. I had assumed this morning she was in her room still hurting.

"I saw her, though," Punky said, still crying, "but she didn't see me."

"Where? When?" I asked him.

"I ain't telling."

"Oh yes you are, or I'm going to whip your butt." He was a stubborn little boy. If only Rhenda was here. "And you don't know where Rhenda is? Rhenda left you here by yourself?"

"No. I think she thought Mama was in the bed 'sleep when she left. She took Tomika someplace."

"And you've been home by yourself all day?" Mama would kill her.

He shook his head yes.

"Oh my God," I said, "I'm going to find Rhenda. Come on."

He shook his head no.

"Boy, don't make me mad at you," I warned. But he looked so pitiful. I tried to hug him and he kept pulling away. Then I heard the screen door open. I jumped up, realizing I hadn't latched it when I came in because I'd run into Punky's room to see what was wrong.

I heard Rhenda almost cooing to the baby like she wasn't two years old. "You my precious baby, Tomika. Say mommy. Say mommy."

Tomika said, "Mommy. I love you, Mommy."

"Rhenda, come here," I yelled, going over to Punky's doorway.

She came in holding Tomika on her hip. "What's wrong with *him?*"

"He's crying about something, but he won't tell me. You in trouble, girl. You left him here by hisself."

"I did not," she said calmly. "Mama was here 'sleep."

I shook my head no.

"What do you mean, no? Did she get up and leave with you?"

"Punky says she left last night and never came back."

"Punky is lying. How would he know? He was dead 'sleep."

"No, I wasn't. I followed Mama," he said, tears running down his face.

"You did what?" I yelled. "Mama is going to whip you good, boy."

"Hold up," Rhenda said. "Where did you follow her to?"

"I can't tell y'all. I just can't."

Rhenda handed Tomika to me and sat down. "Punky. Come on, now. Tell your big sister Rhenda. You know I won't tell Mama on you." She reached out, and he let her hug him.

"Oh, you gon' let Rhenda hug you, huh?" I said.

"Shut up, Keisha. Ain't no time for you to be trippin'. Come on now, Punky. Where did Mama go? Listen. She could have gotten hurt and that's why she's not back."

Evidently he hadn't thought of that. He lifted his head, "First I saw her arguing with Jeebie. Then I followed her to . . . to—"

Rhenda said, "To what, baby? Come on, now. We might have to go look for her."

I had stopped breathing. Mama even talking to Jeebie was a thought that didn't fit into my brain. I waited for Punky to say he followed her to church. Church is the only place Mama has been at night since she got saved.

"I followed her . . . to . . . you promise you ain't going to tell her you know, right? You promise me, Rhenda? You, Keisha?"

I could see this was hurting him, whatever it was. Rhenda said she promised. I didn't say anything, hoping he'd forget about me like he always does. He really only cared if Rhenda was mad at him.

"You ain't say nothing, Keisha?" he said, wiping his eyes.

"Okay, okay. I promise," I said.

"She went into the"—he stammered some more, until it rushed out like three curse words—"the Lion's Den."

Me and Rhenda looked at each other.

"You musta made a mistake," Rhenda said. "Mama wouldn't go into the Lion's Den. Do you even know what that is?"

"I know," Punky said, lifting his head up. "It's where the women dance naked. Me and some of the boys have tried to peak through the window before. I ain't dumb."

The Lion's Den was a black strip joint where women did exactly what Punky said and probably even more. It was open twenty-four hours a day and it was down in the bottom, at the end of a dead-end road in a cinder-block pink building with a big lion on top, and an almost naked woman straddling it. Children couldn't go there. And if they had any sense, they didn't want to. But our own mama being there was not something that I could believe.

Rhenda said, "Okay. Maybe Mama went in there to talk to somebody. I'm sure she knows some of the dancers. I mean some of them live here in these projects."

"Yeah," I said, "you know Mama. She wouldn't be going in there for any other reason. Rhenda's right."

I had to believe Rhenda was right. But I could see the shadow on her face. She wasn't sure herself. Then we heard her—Mama calling us.

Punky looked panicked. "Don't tell her. Please. She'll get mad at me for following her."

Rhenda held her finger up to her mouth and said, "We promise. We're going to act like we don't know nothing. Mama ain't going to know. We just gonna forget this, okay? It's over and it's nothing we can do about it. Mama is grown. Right?"

"Right," I said. "We promise. We won't tell, so dry your eyes and clean up before she starts questioning why you crying, Punky."

Rhenda left first with Tomika. I heard Mama talking to the baby but not Rhenda. Then I heard her say, "I'm tired and I don't feel good. Rhenda, get them something to eat. I'm going to bed."

I rushed out there to see if I could tell where she'd been by looking at her, even though I realized that made absolutely no sense. But I was too late. Mama had already gone in her room and closed the door.

I whispered to Rhenda, "How did she look? What did she have on? Did she smell like she'd been drinking?"

Rhenda said, frowning, "She looked beat. And I couldn't see what she had on because she had on a raincoat. And she was rolling around a breath mint in her mouth."

"A raincoat. As hot as it is? And it ain't raining? What about drinking? Did she smell like she was drinking?" I felt sick myself now. The only reason anybody would have on a raincoat in this heat is because they were trying to hide something. But what? What was Mama trying to hide? A G-string outfit?

"I say we drop it," Rhenda said. "Maybe she just wanted to have a night out on the town or something. She deserves it. Maybe she needed a break. Let's just let her sleep and go on like nothing's happened. We have to anyway. We don't want Punky in trouble, do we?"

"You're right," I said. But I could see Rhenda didn't believe a word Mama'd said.

We ate and went to bed without talking to her. It wasn't usual for Mama to not get up, at least, before our bedtime to say good night. But what can you do? I thought. She's the mama.

Betty was doing pretty good in the hospital. I went to see her as much as I could. "Betty," I said to her when she could talk okay, "I don't want to trouble you, 'cause you got troubles of your own, but I think I have a problem."

"What? You can talk to me. I'm your friend, right?"

"I hope. How did you know your mama was using drugs?"

"Drugs? Who you think is using drugs? Rhenda? I doubt it. That girl ain't using nothing."

"Not Rhenda," I said, afraid I was about to break down crying. "Just a person I know, that's all."

"You mean that bitch Kimmie. You damn straight that girl is a cokehead. You ain't know that? Everybody know that."

I didn't. And I was not sure Betty knew, either. Right now I didn't really care, though. But for the sake of not saying who it really was, I pretended that Kimmie was who I was asking about. "Okay. Let's say she is. What signs could I tell Miss Troutman to look for?"

"Hmm. Well, if she ain't shootin' up, then I'd say, fidgeting, or maybe never sleeping, bags under her eyes. Possibly what look like a sore or a track under one or both her pig nostrils. You know, acting hyper sometimes. Talking bold, bragging, and talking real fast. Of course, with that chick you probably couldn't go by that, 'cause she always think she got it going on. And then some people know how to keep it hid. My mama kept it from us for a long, long time. Now she wide open."

I left Betty with my heart ripped to shreds. I couldn't recall Mama doing any of this, but of course she'd been sleeping most of the time when she was at home lately. Every night that week she was gone out. And every day I lost more and more interest in swimming or going to Avery. I could only wonder what was happening to Mama.

Rhenda put all her energy into cleaning and cooking for us. She had started getting up early when I got up, mopping the kitchen. I'd seen this behavior in her only once before, when she was worried about telling Mama she was pregnant. Sort of a nervous cleaning spree.

We barely saw Mama but when I did see her, she looked tired and worn out. She claimed she'd gotten a night-shift job in a warehouse. And to make it more suspicious, she'd gotten a beeper for us to call her in case of an emergency.

Yesterday, Punky said that he saw Mama take a wad of cash out when she gave him his lunch money. Sometimes Mama cashed her welfare check before she paid the rent instead of using one of those debit cards. Especially if she was late. She'd just pay it in cash. But Punky swears it was way more money than she normally had rolled up. And then one of his friends said they saw Mama arguing with Jeebie on the corner again.

I was scared. My own mama might be selling drugs, hooking, or both. I didn't want to think that, but each day that passed more and more happened that made me wonder. I could face the facts. But could I deal with l-o-w-d-o-w-n?

I had to figure out how to save Mama. One night soon I was going to follow her myself.

There were only two more meets to go. A man connected with the Olympic swimming teams was supposed to be at the last meet just to watch me. Originally it was supposed to be me and Betty, but that was out now. But like all our meets, this one was important to Mr. Walt. In the last few days, he'd had asked me so many times what was the matter, I wanted to vomit. He kept mentioning that I wasn't swimming like I used to.

He'd gotten Clarissa and Phyllis to talk to me before this meet. But I couldn't tell anyone what was bothering me. Normally the only people I couldn't keep a secret from were Rhenda and Mama. So now I had no one to turn to.

At the meet, Malik came over at the last minute. "Hey. What's the matter? Coach says you buggin.'"

"Buggin'? Me. He buggin' for putting you in my business. Ain't nothin' wrong that people leaving me alone won't cure," I said, turning away from him like I was looking for somebody.

Malik said, "Betty told me you been coming to the hospital to see her. Thanks. She getting out tomorrow."

I didn't say nothing.

He tapped me on the shoulder.

I spun around. "What?" I said, almost shouting.

He held both hands up in front of him. "Nothing. Dang. You ain't got to be so touchy. I just wanted to say that I think you're . . . never mind," he said, hunching his shoulders. "You're right. It's your business."

"What? You think I'm what?" I asked him. What did he want to say?

"I was gonna say," he said, moving away from me, "you're a nice girl, that's all."

What did he mean by that? Was he saying I was nice because I'd been visiting Betty? Or did he mean it in another way? I was trippin'. But there was something about the way he was staring at me before he said it that was different. I swam, but now I couldn't concentrate at all. I kept rewinding what Malik said, and why he said it. Twice I scratched on the board, hitting the water before the whistle. In other words, I lost—big time.

"Keisha, what happened out there?" Mr. Walt said. "You could outswim every girl on that team and you come in fourth? Are you sick or something? Is it your hair?"

I frowned. *"My hair?"* I said, looking at him like he must be crazy.

"Yep. You remember. I told you we lose girls on account of the chemicals messing up their hair. This is your big chance. Don't let hair stand in your way."

"Mr. Walt," I said, wrapping my towel around my waist, "you know what? I wish it *was* my hair standing in my way," and walked off.

Mr. Walt called out, "I'm going to come over and talk to your mother if you don't snap out of this. We only have a few weeks to get ready for the Olympics guy."

I turned around and lied, "I'll be ready." But I just didn't care no more. I didn't care that I'd lost at all. And nothing he or anyone else could say, including Mama, would make me care. Not now.

That night when Mama left at 12:30 A.M. I sneaked out of my bed and I left behind her, hiding in the shadows as we moved from one block to the next. She left in her raincoat again. But, at least, this time it was raining. She didn't get on the bus like she was going to work; instead, she turned the corner toward the Lion's Den.

I couldn't breathe when I saw her go inside. The rain had slacked off, and I didn't see her give the man at the door any money. He didn't stamp her hand like he did the men going in. I saw the man peek outside for a second.

I was at the corner, but I figured he might spot me. So I crouched down and ran toward the side of the building. I slid down behind a Dumpster. Either Mama was dancing nude or turning tricks or dealing drugs—or all three. There was no other explanation. I sat down on the filthy, stinking heap of rags and trash laying outside the Dumpster and cried. I cried until I thought my guts would shoot out. I was sho'nuf losing it and I couldn't get a hold of myself.

Then I felt a hand on my shoulder. Startled, I looked up. The man from the door must have seen me? But when I stared into the darkness I could see it wasn't *that* man. This one held up a lighter, and the tiny flame illuminated the Devil's face—Jeebie.

"What you doing back here, sweet-thang?" he said. "What's the matter?"

I swallowed hard. Should I scream? No. Somebody might go get Mama. I tried standing up, but he tightened his hand on my shoulder and shoved me back down. Then in a flash he crouched beside me. He pulled me close to him by my windbreaker. I could smell the alcohol on his breath and I wanted to puke. "Let me go," I gasped. "Please, or I'll scream." His face was a blur through my tears.

"No, you won't. See this?" The glint was unmistakable—a knife. "You a smart girl, a pretty girl. You don't want to get hurt, do you?"

I shook my head no.

"I can't hear you?" he said, and grinned.

I trembled all over. My teeth were chattering. Sweat dripped off my face. "What do you want?" I asked, trying to sound tough.

"I heard all this shit you been saying about me. You been running me down to that ho Betty, right? Saying I wasn't good enough and shit. What do you know about me? Huh? Little bitch."

I didn't want to keep crying. But the tears kept coming. "I ain't said nothing 'bout you to nobody. Honest," I stammered.

"Yeah. Well, it don't matter now, does it? 'Cause you gon' want nobody but Jeebie when I finish. I got it on like that. I'm gonna make you squeal like a pig, girl, just like that freak Betty."

Now I was mad. How dare him talk about Betty. I dug my nails into his hand and tried prying his claw off me.

He hit me. *Wham*.

I'd never been hit by anybody before, not in the face. And my body jerked involuntarily. I said, "Please, please, don't rape me."

"I ain't gon' rape you, bitch. I don't rape women. They want it. Say it. You want me, don't you?"

I hated him. I wanted to kill him. I sure didn't want him touching me, so I decided—I opened my mouth and let out a scream.

He grabbed me, pulled me closer, and put his arm all the way around my neck until his hand was on my face. He clamped his palm over my mouth. He had me in a choke hold, and I could barely move.

My mind raced. How could I make him turn me loose? I imagined him pulling my panties down and, oh God, I wanted to die.

I shook my head as hard as I could to get rid of his

hand. I flung my head back, felt his grip slipping because my face and hair was still wet. I bit down on the side of his hand. He yelped like a hit dog and jerked his hand from my mouth.

I tried stumbling up, but he grabbed me and yanked me back down, hard. He pushed his palms into my chest and shoved me back onto the dirty rags and trash. The rotten smell rushed into my nose. I was choking as we struggled.

He had me by the neck with one hand and he was struggling to pull down my pants with the other, while still holding on to his knife.

He *was* going to rape me. I tried kicking him off me, rolling over, but he was on top of me and he held me down. I squeezed my eyes shut. Death. God, please just let me die now. Right now.

Then I heard it. A crashing sound. I felt Jeebie's grip relaxing. I coughed violently as air rushed into my lungs.

He was off me.

I could move. I scrambled to get my pants up as I tried to stand.

Jeebie and a man were fighting.

The man had Jeebie against the Dumpster, hitting him. I thought, What if Jeebie gets away and comes after me? It was raining again, coming down in big drops. I couldn't really see the man's face. I scrambled around on the dirt, feeling with my hand for the knife. I grabbed it. If Jeebie got free, I would stab him. Not only for me but for Mama too.

He stumbled toward me. The man picked Jeebie up

and flung him down, like he was no more than a sack of potatoes. Then he lifted Jeebie's head and hit him hard one more time in the face. He rolled Jeebie over, clasping one of his arms behind his back. Jeebie collapsed flat on his stomach. His face squished into the dirt. The man reached inside Jeebie's jacket and pulled out a gun. He dropped the bullets from the gun onto the ground and stuck the empty gun into his own pocket.

Then he turned around in the rain. He was wet and muddy from head to toe. For a second I was terrified. Suppose he was as mean and crazy as Jeebie and tried to rape me? I clinched the knife's handle tightly, my fingers aching from fighting with Jeebie.

"Are you all right?" he said. It was Mr. Hakim. "Did he . . . ?"

His question hung in the air for a second. I said, "No. But he was trying to. God, Mr. Hakim, thank you. Where did you come from?"

"Hey, you're okay, right?"

"Yes," I said, breaking into uncontrollable sobs.

"Come on," he said, taking me by the shoulders, helping me up. "I'll get you home."

I hesitated.

"It's okay. I'm cool. Really," he said. "I'll take you straight home, I promise."

I wanted to go home, and I wanted him to go get Mama out of the Den. But how could I tell anyone what she was doing? I looked around, hoping she'd be standing outside. There were a lot of cars in the Den's parking lot. The music blasted so loud from inside, I could see why no one came to my rescue. I could have screamed my head off and probably no one would have heard me. I couldn't tell Mr. Hakim my mama was dancing or doing something worse in there, so I let him help me stagger up the street about a block to his station wagon.

Inside the car, he handed me a blanket. "Here. Wrap up in this."

I handed him the knife and took the blanket. I pulled it around me. I wanted to speak, but I couldn't stop crying or shivering.

"Hey, you can cry on my shoulder if you want to," he said, almost in a whisper.

After Jeebie, I didn't ever want to touch another man or have one touch me. I shook my head no.

He said, "I understand. What I don't understand is what were you doing hanging out with Jeebie at the Lion's Den?"

"I wasn't with Jeebie," I said, feeling like he might as well have slapped me in the mouth with his question.

"Then what were you doing at the Den?"

I couldn't answer him. I shrugged.

"The Den ain't no place for a young girl. Hey, it ain't no place for nobody, really."

I wanted to ask him then, Why were you there? But he told me.

"I drive through almost every night hoping I can dissuade some young woman to give up the trade. Most times I don't get out of the car. I just ride through the parking lot and then leave. But tonight, I don't know. Something told me to go to the door. When I got near it, I felt funny. I heard noises—followed them—and saw you struggling with that creep. At first I didn't want to interfere. I thought maybe you had come freely with him."

"I did not," I said loudly.

"Actually, I wasn't even sure it was you. But then I thought, I don't give a shit, excuse my language. You ain't but fourteen years old. And you ain't old enough to *give* nobody nothing. Leastways not consent. Plus, I ain't watching this go down in front of my face."

I wasn't following everything he said, but I was so happy he came when he did. Otherwise I'd be another statistic. "Do you know what time it is?" I asked him.

"Why? You know your mama is going to be mad at you, right? You know you ain't got no business out here. It's a little after two A.M."

It seemed like I'd been fighting Jeebie off for hours.

"I'm going to take you home," he continued, "tell your mama what happened, and then it's over. She can take you to the police . . . or I can."

"You can't tell Mama," I blurted out.

"Oh, I can," he said. "Trust me."

"I don't want her to know," I said, stammering. I didn't want anyone to know my mama wasn't even home this time of night. And that she was inside the Den, while I'm right outside almost being raped. I pleaded, "I'll tell her what happened, I promise."

He looked at me. "What is up? You hiding something?"

Why would he say that to me? God. This was too complicated. "Could you just take me home?"

"I should take you to the police station," Mr. Hakim said. "That damn, excuse my language, Jeebie has done this before with a young girl I know. She wouldn't turn him in either. No matter what I said. He convinced her that it was on her. That's sick, you know. He's the bad guy here."

"I know," I said, remembering Jeebie saying that I wanted him. I shivered.

"You can press charges against him," he continued. "I *know* he'll never bother *you* again. But that creep needs to go to prison."

"No. I told you, I'll tell my mama. Please, I'll take care of it." I couldn't let Mama know I followed her. I just couldn't face her if she knew that I knew what she was doing. Not tonight, anyway.

"Okay. Okay. Calm down," he said. "I don't want to make you any more upset than you are."

He started the car and took me home. He got out of the car in front of our place. "Hey," he said, following behind me. "Listen to me, Keisha. You can press charges tomorrow. I'll be there for you if you need me."

"I'll think about it," I said, wishing he'd just go away.

"You do that," he said. "And, good luck on your meet."

"What meet?" I turned around and faced him. "I'm finished with swimming."

"Oh. Really. Why is that?" he said.

"What's the point?" I said.

"Hey, don't let them win."

"Them? Them who?"

"Them who think this is all there is. Just don't let

186

them win. Only a dreamer can make a dream come true. In the end, whether you rich or poor, all there is separating you from success is a dream. Here's my card. You ever need anything, anything, come see me. Okay?"

I took the card.

"Sure," I said. "And I'm sorry about not getting in the car at first."

"Hey, no problem," he said, interrupting. "It's better to be safe than dead. I don't have a beef with you not getting in the car with a stranger. After all, I realize I'm a stranger to you. But like I said, anything. Okay?"

I waved good-bye and let myself inside our apartment. I tiptoed into the bathroom and shut the door. There was no lock.

Rhenda barged in while I was taking off my muddy, torn clothes. "What happened to you? Where you been? Mama is going to get you, girl."

"First, Mama can't do nothing to me no more, Rhenda. And I don't want to talk about what happened right this minute. I want to take a bath and go to bed." I wanted to take a shower, too, but we didn't have one.

"I ain't leaving this bathroom till you tell me what happened to you. You got a black eye, your face is all scratched up. Naw. You going to tell me who bothered you and I'm going to wake Punky up and we gon' deal with this tonight."

She wasn't about to leave. I'd have to tell her. The last thing I needed was her to wake Punky up. I told her what happened. Where Mama had gone and how Jeebie tried to rape me.

Rhenda began crying softly.

I hated to see her hurt this way. It was bad enough for one of us to be hurt. "Don't tell Punky, okay? Let him stay innocent for as long as he can," I said.

"You right. I won't tell him. But what about Jeebie? You going to have him up?"

"How? I wasn't supposed to be there, remember? If I have him up, then Mama's gonna know I followed her, and her cat is out the bag too. All I know is I'm hurting everywhere, inside and out. I don't feel like thinking right now."

"It's okay. I'm glad Mr. Hakim showed up. What about tomorrow? You want me to come with you to practice? Punky wants to come anyway. I have enough for bus fare for me and him. You know, just in case Jeebie shows his face. All of us together can take care of him."

"I ain't going," I said, sinking down into the water, wishing I had some bubble bath.

"What? You nuts. Of course you're going. You got to practice every day. What about the man who is supposed to be there next week to look at you and invite you to the winter tryouts. If he doesn't see you swim, you can't go."

"I know all that. I told *you*, remember. I'm just not going. I don't care about it anymore. I don't care about swimming. I don't care about Avery. I don't care. There is nothing to win for. I see it now, Rhenda. We just losers. I honestly thought about not even fighting Jeebie. Just let him rape me and I have his funky baby and forget all this dreaming stuff. It don't work. I'm going to end up disappointed like my sister, like my mama, and everybody else I know."

"Now who ain't making sense? You can't give up. You can't. Hell, all of us just can't give up," she said, crying. "You got to go on, if not for me—what about Tomika?"

"Look. You fight for Tomika. I can barely take care of myself. Now get out. I'm tired."

Rhenda left out, crying. I sank down into the water, deeper and deeper, until it covered up my head. I should drown myself.

Mama was shaking me. "Get up. You late. You've got to practice. The minibus will be out there to pick you up soon."

I pulled the cover over my head. "I ain't going."

"What? Of course you're going," Mama said. "Now get up and get your butt on outta here."

"I'm *not going*. Now, please, Mama. Leave me alone."

She tugged the cover. I pulled it up farther over my head and held tight. Now it came to me that she was going to freak when she saw my face. What could I tell her? Think. I sure couldn't stay in the bed forever. I was so tired when I finally went to bed I forgot about having to explain my face and body all bruised up.

"Rhenda. Get up and help your sister get ready. I'm exhausted and I've got to get some sleep," Mama said sort of in a whisper so she wouldn't wake up Tomika.

Yes, I thought. You're exhausted, all right. Probably drunk too or high off that crack. If I can make it until she walks out, I'm home free—at least, until I can think of something to tell her.

"I'm getting up, Mama," Rhenda said. "Go on to bed. I'll help her. You go on."

Mama shuffled out.

Whew, I said to myself. Rhenda will not let me down, no matter what.

"If I was you," Rhenda said, sitting on the side of my bed, "whether I was going to practice or not, I'd get out of here before Mama sees you."

"Okay. You're right. But I am not going to no practice. So if anyone calls here, you get the phone first."

"I'll try. You know I can't stop Mama from answering her own phone if she decides to, though. Why don't you just go talk to her. Somebody probably going to tell her anyway. You know 'bout how long a secret can stay hidden in this neighborhood."

"I ain't telling her, and neither are you. I'll take my chances," I said, getting up and putting on my clothes as quick as I could. "How is my face?" I asked. We had a dresser in the room but no mirror on it.

"You look like you been fighting Holyfield and he won.

You better hurry up. She gon' know something's up if that minibus blows outside. Maybe you can catch it at the corner and tell them you going to ride the city bus straight to the MLK Center. Make up your mind quick, though. I think I hear Mama still moving around in her room."

I kissed Rhenda on the cheek and rushed out the door. I remembered I'd left my swim bag that had my stuff in it. If Mama woke up and saw it, she'd know I wasn't at the center. I turned to go back in.

Rhenda handed me the bag out the screen door. "Take these too," she said, handing me a pair of black sunglasses, a rayon scarf and some change. "Wait, one more thing, here," she said, handing me a screwdriver. "If anybody mess with you, do it. Now, hurry. She's still up. I told her to clip Tomika's toenails for me. She knows I like her to do that. It ain't going to be long before she's done, though."

I stuck the screwdriver in my jacket pocket and ran. My entire body was in pain. Every step hurt. I stood at the corner waiting for the minibus. I was glad today was Monday. Clarissa didn't drive on Mondays. If she had been driving, she would not only come to my door but insist that I ride with her. This morning it was Kimmie. She never spoke to me anymore, which was a good thing most days, today it was great. She wouldn't care what I did.

I slipped the sunglasses on and wrapped the scarf around my head, tying it under my chin. When the van pulled up, I stepped up to it and mumbled that I was going to be a little late, so I'd catch the city bus.

Kimmie barely looked out and said, "Okay," and

pulled off. Malik wasn't on the van either. I wondered if he was swimming in the meet. Kente had long ago stopped coming to the center. I heard he was hanging out drinking wine at the corner store.

I didn't even look to see if anyone else on the mini-bus was looking back at me. I just started walking toward the basketball court a few blocks away. I sat down on a cement bench. I felt like it was all a big waste. All my struggling, studying. All for nothing. Why me? I could face the truth now. You, Miss Keisha Wright, owe Ms. Hill a big apology. She was the first one to come right out to your face and tell you the truth, you ain't shit, your family ain't shit, and you ain't gon' never be shit.

I'm not sure how long I sat there. A few times guys came over and bugged me. But they soon all left and I was in the park alone, except a few homeless men laying out. I thought, I might as well be homeless. I didn't have any-place to go. But I wasn't homeless, and I'd have to go there sometime. Home? What was I going to tell Mama? A lie? What did it matter? Mama been lying to me all this time. I thought she was all right. She always pretends to be so righteous. Yeah. How you gon' be righteous drink-ing and dancing naked on a stage all night and God knows what else?

My grandma used to say to me, "The darkest hour is gon' come just before dawn." Well, for me and my family, we just plain gon' live in the dark. There ain't no dawn for people like me. Keisha Wright, face it, you born for darkness, you poor and that means only one thing. You were born in sin.

I saw a policeman stop his patrol car and get out. He roused the homeless men. I didn't want him coming over to question me. But where could I go? I didn't hang around with anyone anymore. Betty was home from the hospital, but I wasn't sure about going there. What if Malik saw me looking this way? What about it? He doesn't give a flying monkey about me. I headed toward Betty's. I needed to let her know what Jeebie had tried to do. Maybe that would make her understand what a loser he was, no matter what he had to say.

I could hear the noise and music the minute I walked up to their screen door. I banged on it. After a while, Betty's mama came to the door. She looked worse, skinnier, weaker, and she had on a cut-up pair of jeans. Every vein in her leg was protruding out. It was sad.

"I heard Betty was home," I said. "Can I see her for a minute?"

"Sho'. Come on in. Betty," she yelled, "your little friend . . . what's your name, girl?"

"Keisha," I said, wishing I hadn't come.

"Yeah, that little old gal you think is so damn smart is here. Keisha somebody."

Betty came out in her nightgown. "Hey, what you doing here?"

"What am I doing here? I came to see you. What kind of way is that to say, hey?"

Suddenly I felt scared. What if Jeebie were here? I hadn't thought about that. What if he'd told Betty his own version of last night? No. He wouldn't. She didn't know. But what if he comes over here? But no, Betty *had* to be still pissed at him. And what about her family? Surely they wouldn't let him near Betty. Then I looked at her mama, and the thought surfaced, God, he's probably this woman's dealer.

"Why you got all that shit on, gal?" her mama asked me. "Ain't you hot?"

Betty glared at her and said, "Keisha, come on back here in the room with me so we can talk."

I followed her back into the bedroom. They lived in public housing, like we did. But they didn't keep house like us. Clothes were strewn all over the bedroom. Betty pushed a few shirts off a chair and said, "Sit down. My room is a mess, ain't it? Ain't nobody 'round here can keep nothing clean except Malik. He got his own room and he keeps it like a shrine, flowers and shit everywhere. I used to clean up my room and the rest of the house, but since I got shot I can't do everything. Now, you gon' tell me what is wrong wid you? Why do you have that shit on?"

I sat very still. Should I tell her about Jeebie? No. That would hurt her too bad. What was I thinking? I couldn't tell anyone. I said, "Nothing. I fell, that's all. I hurt my eye and scratched up my face."

"Fell where?" Betty said, looking at me like she knew I was lying.

"In the woods. I was on a camping trip with the center and I climbed up this rock and fell, that's all." When I said it I could feel my shoulders relaxing. That was it. My alibi. Lately, Mama didn't know what we'd been doing at the center. I could just say I went with

Clarissa and Phyllis and fell off a boulder or something. God, I could say a mountain, she wouldn't know.

"I know you lying," Betty said. "So what happened? Give it up."

I took my shades off. If I could convince Betty, I could get Mama. "What does that look like to you? I tumbled down some rocks, hit my face a few times, blacked my eye, and here I am, barely able to move today."

"Uh-uh. Girl. Ain't no rock smacked you in the face like that unless it was in the shape of a fist. Now, who hit you?"

"Nobody. You don't know. Look," I said, standing up, "I didn't come over here for no police questioning. I'm going."

"Please. Don't go. Sit. I promise. No more questions about that," Betty said. "I got some good news."

Thank God. I needed to hear something good. "Tell me, girl. What you waiting for, snow?"

"You ain't gon' trip, right? Don't, because this is too good for you to make me feel bad about it."

I stopped breathing. What was it? Was she pregnant again? Going to run away?

"Me and Jeebie getting married," she said, grinning.

I dropped my head down like it was as heavy as a tractor trailer. At first I couldn't speak. I wanted to cry—no, die.

I got up. "I forgot. I've got to be somewhere in a few minutes." I put my shades back on. I headed to the door.

"Hey, you gon' diss me again like that? Hey, you suppose to be my girl? What is up wid you? This ain't bad. I know you don't like Jeebie, but, hey, nothing could be worse than living here, watching my mama evaporate. Malik and them can take it. But not me. I can't take it no more. Jeebie say he gon' get me my own place. A fancy apartment and a car. Hey, you can hang out wid me some, like old times. We can sit back, chill, drink some forties."

I looked at her, tears spilling onto my face. "Drink some forties? When did you start drinking?" It was the only thing I felt like tackling out of all she'd said. "You mean you sitting up in here watching your mama and daddy die from drugs and alcohol and you gon' drink some forties? I'm outta here."

I ran out, brushed past her mama on the steps. I heard her calling me back. I stopped out of habitual respect for old people. I turned around. "Yes, ma'am."

"Hey girl, what your name?" she slurred. "Can you go get me a rock? That damn daughter of mine, she ain't no good. Old half-white heifer. Just like her old man. Think she too good for me. I been fighting her all morning to get off her ass and call Jeebie. That boy is all right. He look out after his soon to be mama-in-law."

I stared at her. How could she not hate Jeebie after he'd almost killed her own daughter. Then it hit me. "Why did you call Betty that?" I asked her, hoping Betty didn't come outside and find me interrogating her mama. But I had to know why she would say something so mean and stupid.

"Humph. Ha, call her lazy? Hell, 'cause the little ho is lazy. I don't see what a good man like Jeebie want wid her. I told him," she said, slurring, and flicking ashes off her cigarette, "he coulda had me."

I shook my head. This woman was *Nightmare on Elm Street* nuts. "No," I said. "Why would you call her half-white?"

"Hell, her daddy was a no-good cracker. What that make her? Little high-yellow bitch. I can't stand her little young ass. She sweet on my old man too. I told 'em if I catch 'em together, I'm gon' slit her white-ass throat. She swear up and down he like a daddy to her. She always stuck up under Malik. He run my old man off sometimes just 'cause he drunk. That boy, I'm gonna put his ass out. Got all them damn trees and shit growing up in my house like it's a damn farm."

She rambled on. I wanted to run back inside and drag Betty out. I had never heard someone's mother talk about them like that. No wonder Betty wanted to get away. Betty's choices were between monkey shit and donkey shit. Nothing could be worse than your mama talking about you like this. Nothing. I didn't even respond, I merely took off. I walked up the street, thinking about Betty. Was it true? Was she half-white? Is that why she hate white people? She too dark to pass for white, but she know she got their blood in her. That explains her hair and her coloring. Must be her mama had her by someone else while she was with Malik's daddy. I bet knowing that makes it hard for Malik's daddy too. But it must be even worse for Betty. She's trapped inside her own body. Fighting her own self. Betty living in hell.

I walked briskly, trying to get as far away from them as I could. I headed to the small park only a few blocks away. I was feeling confused and angry. I heard a man's voice calling to me. I speeded up. I didn't bother to look back at first. I didn't want to talk to anyone. Then I felt uneasy. What if it was Jeebie? I felt in my coat pocket for the screwdriver. I squeezed the handle in my palm. If he came near me this time, I was ready for him.

The person was not calling anymore, but I could hear their footsteps gaining on me. When they were almost at my heels, I swung around, the screwdriver ready to take out an eye if necessary.

"Hey, it's me. I didn't mean to scare you," Malik said, holding up his hands and jumping back. "I thought you heard me calling. Betty sent me to find you. She said somebody had jumped you."

I lowered the screwdriver. "Sorry," I said, dropping my head down.

"Who did this to you?"

I didn't say anything, just chewed my lower lip. I couldn't cry. Not now. I said, "It's all right. I fell."

"Yeah right, into a fist. Look, I'm just trying to help you."

"Why, what do you care?" I said, not looking up, wondering why I was asking him such a stupid question. My head was throbbing, and I felt like I would pass out any second. I touched my face and felt the swelling.

"You need to sit down. Here," he said, taking off his shirt and laying it on the grass. "Sit down. Just sit and rest a minute."

I didn't want to sit down on his shirt, but I didn't want to fall down either, so I sat on it.

"Hey, what happened to you?" he asked, speaking very softly. "Who did this? Tell me."

I couldn't say anything. I just looked down at the grass.

He put his hand under my chin and lifted my face up. I could feel a tremor coming through his fingertips. My stomach lurched.

"Are you all right?" he asked, almost whispering. "You tell Betty what happened to you?"

I gently moved my face away from his hand and looked back down again. I sat there wishing I could sink into the earth and disappear.

"It's okay," he said, still almost whispering. "You don't need whoever did this, you know. He's a coward. I try to tell my sister that. Ain't no man got a right to hit a woman. But if you don't want to talk about it, it's okay. I don't always like talking either."

I sat there thinking about him and what that meant, him taking off his shirt to let me sit on it.

Then he broke the silence. "You know how I said sometimes I don't like to talk?"

I shook my head yes.

"Sometimes, though, I have to," he said. "Like I need to say, if you're going to swim practice, you're late. But I guess you know that."

"I'm not going to swim practice, not now. Not ever."

"Oh," he said, "I didn't figure you like that."

"Like what?"

"A quitter."

"Well, you're wrong," I said, wishing he would leave.

I wanted to be alone. I felt ashamed and uncomfortable and a little angry that he'd chosen now to pay attention to me.

He got up and walked over to the swing and got on one. "Do you mind coming over here for a second?" he said.

I stood up and picked up his shirt. I walked over and sat on the other swing beside him.

He took his shirt from me and put it on. For a minute he sat there staring off into space. "You know, when I was a kid," he said, "I used to come to this park and watch the other kids. I couldn't been more than five or six. Most of them my age, would be with an adult. Not me. My mama, hey, I wouldn't know where she was. And my old man, my real daddy, he was off playing music, so I ain't hardly see him. Anyway, I'd watch the little kids swinging. Usually their mama or daddy would be swinging them and they'd be acting like it was the most fun in the world. When everyone would leave I'd sneak over to the swings. I'd sit here wishing for somebody to swing me up into the air like those kids. But one day when I was sitting here, just watching this scrawny bird flying from tree to tree, I realized there wasn't nobody *to* swing me—except me. So I pushed my feet back in the swing like this," he said, showing me how he'd done it, "and then I just lifted my feet up and *bam*, I was in the air. I kept going farther and farther back before I'd lift my feet, until man, I was swinging just like them kids all by myself."

I waited for him to say more, but he didn't. He just swung back and forth, going higher and higher, grinning.

"And this relates to me how?" I said.

He stopped abruptly, his feet skidding on the ground, dust flying up. He looked directly into my eyes.

My stomach lurched again.

"Sometimes there is no one to swing you," he said. "So you just got to swing yourself."

"Okay," I said, a half smile on my face. "I see your point." Actually I was really feeling surprised and confused that he was talking to me this way. Was this just a brotherly type thing?

"Can I tell you something?" he asked.

"Sure," I said, wondering if he was going to talk about him and Clarissa.

"I work after school as a gardener. And I go to school at night. You didn't know that, did you?"

I shook no.

"I also am learning sculpture. I love it. It's my dream, to one day come to a park just like this, in a neighborhood like this, and with my bare hands hew beauty out of waste. And I am going to do it. I'll plant a beautiful garden and have my sculpture right in the center for the kids. Kids gotta know that all the beauty in the world belongs to all of us. Everybody."

I couldn't believe he was talking to me like this. I knew now what Clarissa meant by saying he was full of surprises. I wanted to ask him, did he go with Clarissa? But I didn't. I just said, "That sounds real nice."

Then he got out of the swing and walked in back of me. "I've seen you swim, girl. You're the best *I've* ever seen. And whenever you ready you can win. Or, you can give up," he said, placing his hand in the middle of my back. "Just remember one thing," he said, pushing me gently, so gently, I could barely feel his hand as I swung up into the air. "I'll be here for you when you need me. But only if you don't let them win."

"Them who?" I asked, closing my eyes and letting the wind whisper on my face.

"Them who would hold you back," he said. "Keisha . . . " He stopped the swing with both his hands on either side of me. He leaned in close to my ear and whispered, "Keisha, don't let them win. I've gotta go now, but if anybody bothers you again, I'm taking it up."

He walked away, leaving me sitting in the swing, almost dazed. I thought, Malik is as gentle as I remember my daddy used to be. It is my only memory of my daddy. Him handing me a teddy bear and gently squeezing my hand. I'm not sure where I was or why he did it. I don't even know how old I was, because Mama swears it didn't happen. But I know it did. I closed my eyes and wished I had a daddy to run to. I finally got up and walked toward home. Yeah, it was easy for Malik to talk about swinging himself. He was a guy. No one tried to rape him. His mother was on drugs, but he didn't have to stay there and deal with it. He could escape with Clarissa. And what was all that he was saying? He must be thinking of me as his little sister or something. God. Forget Malik. What was *I* going to do?

When I got almost to our door, I could see that Mr. Walt's car was sitting out front. I quickly turned around. But it was too late.

Mama yelled, "Keisha. Keisha. Get in here this minute."

Shoot. Mama was standing out on the stoop. If I kept going, she'd come after me. I might as well deal with this, I thought. I walked back and moved past her without saying a word. I came in and plopped down on the sofa, my shades and scarf still in place. I slumped down and prayed I was invisible.

I could sense Mr. Walt sitting across the room in a chair, staring dead at me.

Mama slammed the screen door shut. She had her hands on her hips. "Keisha Wright, where have you been all day?"

"Out," I said, hoping she wouldn't slap me across my face. I'd only seen her hit Rhenda once. She'd whipped us before with a belt and even with a switch if she was really mad. But hitting us in the face wasn't something she did. Until Rhenda cursed her. I thought I was going to have to call the police to get her off Rhenda.

"Out?" she said, making her voice shrill. "Out. I know you ain't telling me that for no answer. And take them shades off and that scarf. Are you crazy, as hot as it is?"

I didn't move or open my mouth. I thought about her deceitful behind wearing a raincoat.

She stomped over toward me.

I took a deep breath and braced myself for the slap.

Instead, she ripped the sunglasses off my face. I heard her catch her breath, her hands flying up to her mouth. Then she said, "What in the name of God happened to you? My Lord. Who did that to you?"

"No one," I said, biting my lip. "I fell."

"You fell, my ass. Who hit you? You better come up with a name," she said, then, taking a deep breath, she yelled, "Rhenda get your behind in here *now*."

I was in trouble. I couldn't use the only alibi I'd thought up since Mr. Walt was sitting quietly watching me. He knew I hadn't been hiking. I was going to have to say something. Mama was getting fired up. I didn't want her to do this in front of Mr. Walt.

"Mama. Please. I'll tell you later," I said, hoping the tears running down my face would soften her up.

Rhenda walked in the room holding Tomika. She didn't say anything. She looked at me to get a cue as to what I was planning. Rhenda would never sell me out. Not even to Mama.

Mama paced the floor, wringing her hands, "Keisha, you are about to make me mad. Now don't make me go off on you in here. I want to know who hit you. And whoever it is, they going to jail—today. So you better tell me."

Rhenda said, "Mama, maybe she can tell you after Mr. Walt leaves."

"No. Mr. Walt ain't going nowhere. If it wasn't for Mr. Walt, hell, I wouldn't even know the girl don' skipped swimming and been hanging out all day. This is not like you, Keisha," Mama said, her voice cracking. "I can't let this happen. Walt. You know that, don't you. I can't let nobody bother my girls. Oh, God. I'm going to have to kill somebody. This can't happen no more."

Mr. Walt stood up. "Listen. This is not the same thing. You going to have to let that go and see what's happening here—now. You don't have to kill anyone. Let the police handle this. Times have changed. Keisha," he said, looking at me, "please, tell your mama who did this. Let her call the police."

Mama stepped in front of me. "Are you using drugs or something? What? You hanging with some pimpish Negro somewhere? You protecting his ass?"

"Mama," Rhenda said, drawing in her breath. "You ain't got no right to talk to Keisha like that. She ain't done nothing wrong."

"Really," Mama said, whipping around toward Rhenda. "So you knew this already? Have you gon' crazy? Both of you?" Then she turned back to me. "Keisha, you know I don't like nobody keeping no secrets in my house."

That was it. I jumped up, moving fast toward the door. "Secrets! You don't want no secrets, Mama. That's what you saying? What about you? You keeping deep, dark secrets. So that's how it is, you can but we can't? That's it?"

"What in the hell are you talking about? You better get back over here and sit down."

"No. Not this time," I said, and I ran out of the house. I ran so hard that it sounded like it was thundering behind me. I didn't even look back to see if she was following me. I would never go back. Never.

I would run away from home. Live on the streets. What else can I do? My mama can't help me. But then it hit me. She was trying to. At least she ain't never talked to me like Betty's mama talk to her. God, I don't know how you can go on breathing with your mama filling you with that kind of venom every single day. No. Mama, she just got a drug problem. Maybe, for a change, I quit thinking 'bout myself. What is happening to my mama ain't her doing. It's that sorry Jeebie's fault or somebody like him. Well, I ain't gon' let Jeebie and no other drug dealer take my mama from me.

When you are backed into a corner with no place else to go, fighting is what works. Not physical fighting, but taking control. My grandma and Mama always say you got to take control or life will control you. How many times had I said that to Rhenda? To Betty? I was not a quitter. Malik was right at least about this.

I will save my mama.

I fished Mr. Hakim's card out of my pocket. His place was in the neighborhood, except it was farther than I could walk, especially as sore as I was. I had the money Rhenda gave me. I rode the bus to his address in an old building that had been renovated. His name was on a small plaque that said, SAVE THE FUTURE. I realized once again I didn't even know his last name. It wasn't on the card. People in the community called him either Mr. Hakim or Keem. His last name on the plaque was DIN. Hakim Din. I walked up the flight of steps to his offices. Inside were five or six girls sitting on straight-back chairs. A woman sat behind a desk. I walked over to her. "Excuse me, but could I see Mr. Hakim, please?"

She nodded. "Fill this out," she said, and handed me a one-page form on a clipboard.

"I'm sorry," I said. "But this is personal."

She looked up and smiled. "They are all personal."

What did she mean? I also realized I knew nothing about Mr. Hakim, really, so why did I think he could help me? I gave her back the clipboard. "Excuse me. But if you don't mind, what does he do?" I asked her.

She said, "He saves young women from a life of prostitution, mostly. Every now and then it's someone just down on their luck. It's okay. We don't judge here. You can fill it out. No one will see it but us."

I stepped back. Did she think I was a prostitute? I said, "I'm *only* fourteen."

She squinched up her face and smiled. "Okay," she said, shaking her head, "so you don't call yourself a prostitute. That's fine. Still, I'll need you to fill this out." She handed me the clipboard back.

I gave up and sat down. I filled it out. Hey, I *was* after all down on my luck. I noticed then at least two of the girls waiting were my age. I was pretty sure one was Hispanic after hearing her talk. The other girls were black.

Mr. Hakim strolled out with a woman in the shortest skirt I'd ever seen. She had tattoos of different-color dragons on one of her arms.

When he saw me he smiled. "I'm glad to see you came here."

I burst out crying. I didn't mean to. But I became a blubbering idiot right then and there.

He said to the other girls, "Do you mind if I see her first? She's having a rough time."

They all chimed no.

I followed him into his office. It was comfortable. He had Native American stuff on the walls. African statues on the coffee table. A desk. A brown leather couch. And two leather wingback chairs. A box of Kleenex sat on the table. He picked up the box and passed it to me. "Here."

I took it and pulled out a few tissues and blew my nose.

"Please, sit down," he said, motioning to one of the wingback chairs.

I sat down. I couldn't talk for crying, but I wasn't even sure what I wanted to say anyway.

"One of my buddies called me. He says your mama is down at the police station raising hell, excuse my expression."

"*What?*" I said. This was worse than I could have imagined.

"Your mama is not one to give up, at least not when it comes to her children. He tells me she's swearing she's going to get someone locked up for smashing your face in. Even the wrong person."

"What do you mean?"

"I mean she's making out a list of suspects. All the boys she's ever heard you mention that you liked. My friend says somebody told your mother they saw a guy talking to you today in the park. They think it was Betty Shabazz's brother, Malik, and that landed him on the top of the list."

"No!" I said, jumping up. "She can't do that. It wasn't Malik."

"Hey, calm down. *I know that*, remember. But she doesn't. I asked my friend to stall your mother. He's not handling this, but he said, of course, the police who are handling it are stalling on principal. So, what you want to do? Let the innocent suffer while you hide out?"

"But if I report it, the police gonna find out I was at the Lion's Den. I got to say where it happened, right?"

"Yes. You'll need to tell the truth. So what?"

"Then Mama will know I followed her. I can't let her know that."

"You don't have a choice. You were right to come here," he said. "I'll go with you to turn the bum in."

I shook my head. "This is so beat up. I didn't come here 'bout Jeebie. I came to see if you could help my mama. She's dancing nude at the Lion's Den and maybe using drugs. All I know is I have to find her some help. I don't care 'bout Jeebie or anyone else. Just my mama."

He leaned forward in the chair. "Keisha, you're wrong. Your mother wouldn't do that. She's *not* using drugs. She wouldn't do any nude dancing. Trust me on this."

"You don't understand," I said. But I wasn't going to argue with him. "Everything is messed up," I said. "Jeebie is out there getting engaged to my best friend. And Rhenda, well, she don' screwed up her life already. Turning Jeebie in ain't gonna help."

"First, feeling sorry for yourself does help—to a point," he said. "But, I can assure you, you can't run away. Trouble will hunt you down and find you, no matter where you hide. As for your mother, hey, she ain't dancing nude or using any drugs. I'd bet my life on it."

"You don't know. She's been fronting," I argued, grimacing to hear the admission spoken out loud. "Everybody think she this upright churchgoing woman who loves her kids. I thought it too. But now I know better. You don't understand. You can't trust her. She will lie. Drug addicts know how to lie good."

"Okay. If that's the truth, what are you going to do?

Become just like her? Start living her life too? Living a lie? What's it going to be? Either you like that kind of person or you don't. People do not become the people they hate unless they despise and hate themselves. I wouldn't have suspected you were that kind of person, Keisha. But hey, what do I know? I'm just plain old dumb, I suppose."

I stood up and started walking around. I guess Mama's pacing is hereditary. I checked out some of the awards he had hanging on the wall, while I thought about what he'd said. I stopped and reread the diploma for his master's degree. His first name was Hakim. But the last name printed on it was Wright. Hakim Wright. I said, "Are you a Wright too?"

He nodded. "Once."

"Oh, are you related to us? I mean to my daddy?" This was a stupid question. There were lots of black people around named Wright.

He cleared his throat. "You could say that I knew him."

"Mama said he died, but me and Rhenda we don't believe her. Do you happen to know where he is?" I thought, This is it. I can run away to my daddy.

"I think you should ask your mama if you want to know where your daddy is. That's how it works. Now, I've got clients out there, so what do you want to do? I'll drive you to the police so you can calm your mama down. If I were you, hey, I'd turn Jeebie in. But I'm not you."

I sat back down and laid my head back, squeezed my eyes shut, and pretended I was getting ready to jump into the water. That was what life was like. Sometimes you dive off the board and hit the water so hard, the air explodes out of your lungs. Suddenly you go sinking down only to spring back up out of the water to catch your breath. Swimming. I didn't mind that it sometimes hurt when I entered the water at the wrong angle or that my nose filled with so much water I nearly strangled. Nothing took that wonderful feeling of freedom away. If Grandma was here, she'd say, "Turn that damn Jeebie in and tell your mama to quit that job and get her act together. Nothing is more important than saving your own family and your own self."

I got up. "I'll go down there. I ain't saying I'll turn Jeebie in, but I'll go get Mama."

"Let's ride, Clyde," he said, smiling. "You don't even know who Clyde is, do you? Never mind. You're too young."

At the police station Mr. Hakim said he'd wait outside. But, he added, if I needed him, he'd be right there
sitting in his car or standing near it. "I get restless sitting
sometimes," he said. Then he nodded. "Go on. Get your
mama."

When Mama saw me walking in, she ran up and
hugged me. "You scared the living life out of me, girl.
Where have you been? What has gotten into you? Whoever hit you musta knocked the sense out your head. But
they gonna pay."

"Mama," I said, "you squeezing too tight. I can barely
breathe." I needed some space between us or I was going

to burst into pure hysteria. "Mama, it's over about who hit me. I just want to forget it."

A woman cop who stood near Mama said, "Well, what if he does it again? And what if he does it to some other girl? Maybe you could be the one to stop this animal, kid. You look pretty beat up to me. I'd take him down if I was you."

Mama said, "How did you know I was here anyway?"

"A friend told me," I said. "Mama, can you walk over here so I can talk to you alone?"

"Sure, baby. And I'm sorry about yelling at you earlier today. And about the things I said. Rhenda is right. You ain't never give me no call to think you was using or hooking. Never. I was out of line. You forgive me?"

"Yeah, Mama. But let me talk, okay. If I turn this guy in, I've got to admit to something myself. It hurts me to tell you. And God knows I wish hadn't found out your secret, Mama. But just let *me* help you for a change. I realize maybe you doing this 'cause of me, Rhenda, and Punky worrying you too much. But we going to stop it. We gon' to start helping out more. I'll make sure Tomika doesn't cry if Rhenda's busy. I'll get a job to help you out. I can work half a day and go to school. I'm not taking college prep anymore ever. And I ain't swimming no more."

"What are you talking about? You ain't going to take no job. Hell no."

"Mama, please," I said, beginning to cry. "Don't make me say it. I don't know if I can bear to say it."

"Say what? All I know is you ain't getting no job. Kids ain't got no 'count to work. Your job is to go to school and get good grades. Get your education. I know what you gonna do. You taking college prep and going to Avery, just like we planned. Whatever it is you've done, forget it. It's over. Ain't nothing you can do that will make me agree to letting you give up your dreams. Too many people in this family don' gave up their dreams already."

"Mama—*I know*."

"Know?" she said, stepping back and holding me at arm's length. "What is it you know? Wait—wait a minute. Who brought you up here?"

"Mr. Hakim."

"Shit," she said.

"It's okay. He just dropped me off. He's not the one who hit me."

"I know damn well he didn't."

"Mama," I said, feeling frustrated. "Are you going to let me talk?"

"Yes, come on over here and let's sit down. I sure didn't want you to find out this way."

"Mama, I'm sorry that I followed you. I shouldn't have, but after Punky saw you and—"

"Punky saw me?"

"Mama, you said I could talk. Punky told us about you having a wad of money. He saw you having an argument with Jeebie and then after that he followed you. He saw you, Mama. And it just about killed him. He was so hurt. He followed you to the Lion's Den."

I saw her about to speak, but I held my hand up. "Let me finish. Anyway. You started staying out late, coming in later. Then I decided to follow you, Sunday night. I saw you go in the Lion's Den to dance nude. I ain't stupid. I know the women in there get high, and work on the side. I hid behind the trash Dumpster. And that's when Jeebie attacked me and tried to rape me."

Mama jumped up. "What? Jeebie. I will kill him. Jeebie tried to rape you? Did you fight him off? How did you get away? *Did he rape you?* Tell me. You can tell me."

"No, Mama. He tried, but he didn't. That's how my face and arms got all scratched up. Then Mr. Hakim jumped on him and beat him up. Mr. Hakim brought me home when I wouldn't go to the police."

Mama sat back down. "Thank God. Thank God." She was crying now. Squeezing my hand, chanting to God, "I know you wouldn't let that happen to my girls. No, God."

The woman police officer came over. "Miss? Are you two all right?"

"Yes," I said. "And I'm ready to tell who beat me up and tried to rape me. I do want to press charges." I had made up my mind. I was not going to let Jeebie win, that's for sure. If me and Mama was going out like this, so was he.

The officer took me into another room. She found two more women to come in. One was a rape counselor. They asked me a million questions. They took photos. And then they said I could go. The cops would be picking Jeebie up. They'd go back to the crime scene looking for evidence and they'd question Hakim Din.

When I found Mama, she was sitting with Mr. Hakim.

"Carolyn told me," he said, patting me on the shoulder.

"That's a brave thing you did, Keisha. The fool should have been locked up a long time ago."

We rode home with Mr. Hakim in silence. When we got home, Mama told him if he didn't mind, she needed to talk to us. He nodded and said he'd call her later.

"No. I want you to come in too," she said. "I think I want you to hear what I have to say."

I was surprised but hopeful. Maybe Mama was going to admit to her drug use and ask Mr. Hakim for help.

Mama said, "I want you all to sit down and listen carefully to everything I'm going to say. No talking and no asking questions until I'm finished."

We all sat down.

Mr. Hakim said, still at the door, "If you don't mind, I'd like to stand. This way I won't be in the way."

"Suit yourself," Mama said, turning back to us.

Tomika stretched her little hands out for me to take her, and I did. Punky sat so close under me, I thought I might smother him. He whispered, "I love you," and smiled up at me.

"My own mama told me I was making a mistake," Mama began, "not telling y'all everything and at the same time making you not keep secrets from me. Now y'all are on my same path, and it's no one's fault but mine."

Mama glanced back at Mr. Hakim.

"No, Mama," I said. She cut me off.

"First, I have not been nude dancing, using drugs, or hooking. I have been going to the Lion's Den at night to keep their books. I used to have a good head in math, plus I started taking an accounting course during the day.

"I didn't tell you for my own reasons. I was ashamed to be a churchwoman and be seen *near* the Lion's Den, to tell the truth. And I wanted this to be a surprise when I came home and announced that your mama had a job in an office somewhere after I finished my course. Plus, I was working to save up money for Keisha so she could go to Avery in the fall."

"You mean you ain't on drugs or nude dancing?" Punky said.

"Didn't you just hear her say that," I said, feeling so relieved I was crying. "Mama, I'm sorry. I should—"

"Let me finish. After the Avery meeting I realized I was being stubborn. There was no way I could save up that much money in time. So I called up the woman and worked out a payment plan.

"As for the money your brother saw me with, I make the deposit for the Den, but a couple of times I've had to bring it home at night because that idiot owner forgets his key to the cash drawer. I deposit it for him at the bank the next day.

"Now, Keisha, I'm proud of you for dreaming big dreams and not giving them up. I knew someone like that myself once upon a time. He tried to tell me that you could be black and have big dreams that came true. But I wouldn't or just couldn't believe it.

"Hakim, please," Mama said, turning around again to him. "Sit down for a second."

Mr. Hakim shook his head no.

I wondered why Mama was making him listen to this. He looked so uncomfortable. I said, "Mama. Let him leave. He didn't do nothing."

"I know that. He can listen to this, though. I want him to hear it."

Then Mama looked straight at Rhenda. "I shouldn't have let you quit school or stay here with Tomika without having a plan for your own future. But I did. I'd given up. Deep down inside ever since I was a young girl like you, I believed that we'd never get out. None of us. I was wrong," she said.

We were all crying. Even Tomika, who hardly ever cried, was crying, though I'm sure she didn't know why. I suppose she couldn't stand to see Rhenda cry.

I said, "Mama, it's okay. You don't have to say no more. It's over now." I didn't want her to say it. To confess what she'd been through. I just wanted to forget it. Because I *had* given up. She had nothing to be proud about.

"No, let me finish," she said, sniffling. "See, I had let the person I hated most in the world rule my thinking for all these years and the day Walter, your Mr. Walt, came in here, I realized that person had won. Walter didn't say it, but I saw it—in his eyes. He knew this person and what he'd done to me, because the man was his uncle.

"See, when I was a little girl, Mama's friend who lived next door, Walter's aunt, Miss Sally, used to always let me spend the night over there. By the time I turned twelve, her husband had started molesting me and making me keep it a secret."

"What?" Mr. Hakim said, in almost a whisper.

I stopped breathing. My mind scrambled into mush. Why was Mama saying this now? In front of *him*—and Punky? It wasn't right. At that moment I realized I didn't like men and now I could see why. They were all alike. I pushed Punky's hand off me.

"You've got to understand, back then it was different. People thought girls who got bothered did something to invite it. I thought it too. He told me if I told, he'd make Mama think I'd been fast with him. He claimed that it would kill my mama, and his wife both, and I'd still be left with just him to take care of me. I was a kid. I didn't know any better.

"You should have told somebody. God," Mr. Hakim said, spinning around in the floor, hitting his hat on his pants. "Damn. I should have known. That's why you were—"

"Hakim, please. Let me finish," Mama said. "By the time I was thirteen I knew better. And I told on him. At first nobody believed me. Then your Mr. Walt came forward and told how he'd seen his uncle pulling me into the shed—but at the time he didn't know what was happening. For a while after, Mr. Walt's family turned on him for telling. We moved, but not until Mama tried to blow the uncle's head off with a shotgun. Luckily she was a bad aim, and it got him in the leg.

"Anyway, after that, I still felt like I was nothing, nobody but scum. So even though I was smart once I got in high school I didn't believe I could make it. I hadn't been smart enough to keep this man from molesting me."

"You were a kid, for God's sake," Mr. Hakim said.

"Then I met your daddy. Rhenda, you and Keisha's daddy. He was smart and sweet but real ambitious. I forced him to get married when I got pregnant with you,

Rhenda. He loved kids and he wanted everything for you. He started working and going to school at the same time. I felt neglected so, before he could graduate, I got pregnant with Keisha. It hurt him because he felt he couldn't afford two children. He graduated high school and got a scholarship to a big fancy college. All paid for. I stayed on here with Mama. He'd come back home, excited, talking about all our dreams. I couldn't see it. I hadn't dreamed a dream since I was a child, before Ms. Sally's husband. Funny, I can't even recall his name, just his ugly old face.

"Anyway, me and your daddy broke up. He didn't want to—I left him. I told him to please let me raise my children alone. My own way. I *wanted* to break his heart like I thought he'd broken mine—and it did. He went to school for a few years. Then I heard he had a nervous breakdown. About two years after that I heard he'd gotten well, gone back to school, and graduated with honors. Sometimes, he'd call me and beg me to let him see you two, but I refused. I told him I'd taught you all that he was dead and if he came around, he'd only confuse you. And now all my secrets are out. I didn't want you to have to deal with no man in your life."

Me, Rhenda, and Punky were crying still. Only Tomika smiled now.

Mama took Tomika out of my arms. "I'm so sorry," she said.

"It's all right Mama. God, I'm just glad to know you ain't stripping and on drugs. What about your argument with Jebbie?"

"He was trying to sell me drugs, so I cursed him out. I

knew Jeebie when he wasn't so trifling. He don't mess with me. And he know I ain't never used no drugs."

Punky looked up. "I love you, Mama. And I love my sisters. But who is *my* daddy? I want to know about my daddy."

I squeezed him around the shoulder.

"Your daddy *is* dead," Mama said. "He's a man I met and dated. He was a nice man, a little older than me. His name was Charles, like yours, Punky. He worked at the post office. He had a heart attack and died before I even told him I was pregnant. I thought it was best not to talk about him. He would have loved you for sure, though," Mama said. "Come on over here, boy, and give me my hugs and kisses back."

Punky went to Mama and hugged her. "I miss having a daddy," Punky said.

"I know, baby. I know," Mama said, rubbing his head.

"Excuse me," Mr. Hakim said. "Do you want me to go now?"

I looked up. I forgot he was in the room. Then I realized it was because he knew me and Rhenda's daddy. Maybe Mama was going to let him tell us where our daddy lived. I repeated his name in my mind, Malcolm Wright. "Yeah, Mama," I said, "you told us about our daddy. Are you going to tell us where he is if he's not dead?"

Mama looked stunned. She said, "I thought you said you knew already, Keisha."

"No, I didn't say that. When?"

"You said Hakim told you everything, right?"

"I said Mr. Hakim told me about you. That he'd bet you weren't using no drugs. And he told me he knew my daddy, that's all. He said I should ask *you* about him."

"My God. I told you all about your daddy because I thought you knew," she said, sighing. Then she shrugged and said, "Hakim did tell you he knew him, huh?" She stared at Mr. Hakim. "What else did he say?"

"Nothing," I said quickly. I didn't want Mr. Hakim to be in trouble. "Just that he's kin to our daddy, too. He didn't tell me who he was."

She said, "Hakim. Hakim is right. He is kin to your daddy, that's for sure. He *is* your daddy. His name wasn't Hakim then. It was Malcolm. He changed his name in later years. He moved back here to be able to watch after you from a distance since I wouldn't let him meet you. He offers me money for you almost every week, *but you know me*—stubborn. I don't take it."

I couldn't move. Hakim Din. I felt confused, betrayed, and torn inside. All this time and he didn't tell me. Didn't say one word.

Rhenda squeezed my fingers in her hand and whispered, "We got us a real daddy, girl."

"Not me," I said, "I ain't got no daddy," and stormed out of the room.

I been in here ever since. I only let Rhenda bring me my food, but I don't talk to her. And I don't even look at Mama. I've heard *that man* in there talking, but they know not to let him stick his head in my room—if he wants to keep it.

224

That man tricked me. He could have just told me the truth. All that time making like he was just a good friend. The whole block probably knew.

Hakim. Hakim Din was our daddy. Well, not mine. I refused to hear it. I closed my ears when Mama said it. He was a skeleton to me too. I was surrounded by skeletons; Mama and Mr. Hakim, they were no different than Ms. Hill and Miss Troutman. What is it that makes people do the wrong things for the right reasons?

25

"Betty! Who let you in?" I asked her, furious. "I told Mama I don't want to see or talk to anyone and I mean it."

"You don't mean me, though—right, girlfriend?" she said, shutting the bedroom door.

"You and anybody else."

"You trippin', girl. Why you got your sister and her baby sleeping on the couch for two days? That ain't you."

"You don't know me. Got it? I'm like everybody else in this world. I'm doing what's best for me. It don't matter to me no more about nobody else's feelings. So please leave." I pulled the covers up over my head.

Betty pulled them down. "Girl, I'm the one should be pissed. You don' broke up my marriage, sent my man to jail, and now I'm all alone. And you trying to say you don't want to be my friend no more?"

I turned to look at her. Was she crying? Nope. But Betty didn't deserve no more grief. "I suppose you could say that. I am *sorry*, Betty," I said, wishing that she'd just go away. At least Jeebie was locked up. It turned out that the bullets *that man* had dropped from Jeebie's gun onto the ground at the Dumpster were important. The bullets matched the one they'd pulled out of Betty.

"You a piece of work," she said. "Come on, get up."

"Quit now. I *said* I was sorry, Betty. I didn't want to hurt you. I, I . . . " I was choking up, my eyes stinging with tears. I had no call to be mad at her, really. She hadn't done nothing. Out of everyone Betty was the only truthful one. She ain't pretending to care about people. She ain't lied about who she is. She just plain Betty.

"Girl, you loco'. Come on. Let's get out of here," she said, yanking the cover again. "What, you gon' stay in here forever? You got your mama out there crying her eyes out. Rhenda thinking she betraying you for sticking up for your mama? What? What you want?"

"I want you out," I said, and turned back over. I didn't really want to be mean to her. But I hated them all. Everyone. Here I was thinking my mama was different. A good, straight-up person. A what-you-see-is-what-you-get kind of person. And then she might as well slapped me in the face.

"I made this bracelet for you," Betty said.

I turned to face her but made no attempt to take the bracelet.

"Here" she said, laying it on my forehead. "I won't take this one back. It's gon' look stupid on your head, though."

"Thanks," I said, still not reaching for it, even though it was annoying up there on my forehead like that.

"Tell me something," she said. "When'd you get so self-ish. Rhenda out there all shook up. She saying you ain't never shut her out like this. So let me understand, you doing all this—why? Just 'cause your mama lied to you. Girl, if I had a dime for every lie my mama told, I'd be rich."

"Your mama is sick," I mumbled.

"And you think what your mama don' is what? Mean? What? Crazy? Rhenda says your mama told you she been confused about what happened to her ever since she was eleven years old. She was so confused, she gave up a *good* man for what—to prove he didn't love her. She is con-fused out of her mind, girl. Hell, I'm fifteen and I stay confused. What you want from *her?*"

"I don't want nothing now. Now that I know she ain't no different from Ms. Hill, Miss Troutman, and the rest."

"You're lucky."

"How's that?" I asked, frowning, refusing to follow her with my eyes back and forth across the room.

"You've got a good family. A mama that loves you. And now you got a daddy that loves you too. Rhenda say he talking about giving you money for school."

She was getting on my nerves, "I'll never use a penny of his money. I ain't going to school or nowhere else. This is where I belong in life. Here. Stuck."

"Huh?" Betty said, pulling a chair up close to the bed and sitting down. "At least your daddy wants to be in your life. Me. What I got? My daddy was so ashamed that he ran off the day I was born and ain't never come back. Look, you can be mad at your daddy forever if you want. But it's your mama who kept him away. And that wasn't really her fault. She mixed up worse than you. Think on it," she said.

"Don't talk about my mama," I said, feeling stupid and more confused to be taking up now for the very person I was mad at most.

"She thinking all men are the same. But they ain't. Punky, he ain't like that. My brother Malik, he ain't like that. And your daddy, from what Rhenda told me, he ain't like that. Now, I got to go. Hey, you don't know what it means to have someone who brought you here to love you. Give your mama *and* daddy a break." She shook her head. "You have no idea what you're doing shutting yourself in here. You better quit trying to drown with me, girlfriend."

I didn't say anything. What could I say? It was the closest thing to feelings I'd ever heard her say. I sat up and hugged her. And wondered if what she said about Malik could be true or was she just trying to make me feel better?

She hugged me back. Then she pushed me away. "Don't get all mushy now. I got to go home and find me a *good* husband this time. Or, maybe I take Malik's advice and take care of myself."

"You can stay here," I said, without even thinking about it.

She looked at me, still no tears in her eyes. "Thanks. I'm outta here," she said, and left.

I wanted to go after her. But I let her go. Would Mama take her in? God, there wasn't enough room for *us*. I just hated the thought of her going home.

"Oh," she said, stepping back into the room. "I forgot. My brother asked me to give you this." She handed me a folded letter. "Don't trip on him, okay. He got enough problems."

I opened the letter and read it.

Dear Keisha, I ain't pushing you. I know what Jeebie tried to do to you. And I'd have hurt him bad had I been there. No. This ain't about that. I just want to hold you. I been waiting to hold you. God, girl. You beautiful. You smart, and I been thinking you needed somebody better than me. But then Betty said for me to let you see the inside of me. She said you were a dreamer and a believer too.

And then, when I saw how you was not letting Jeebie get away, and still going on, I knew, Betty was right. Believe me, I ain't wanting to be with you like in no bad way. Just maybe walk you home from school. Carry your books like my mama says my daddy used to do when they were young. Maybe call you at night and talk to you until I fall asleep. But I ain't wanting to change your plans for college. Nothing like that.
Your man, Malik

I squeezed the letter to my chest and cried, reading it over and over again.

As I read the letter for the twentieth time, I heard Punky outside busting a gut, laughing. I pulled back the curtain by the bed to tell him to get away from the window. He was down on his knees in the dirt doing something. I know he wasn't stupid enough to shoot craps around Mama. I got ready to tell him he'd better quit before he got in trouble. He could hang out with the dumbest boys sometimes. I strained to see what he had in his hands. He was playing marbles. Marbles? I didn't even know he knew what marbles were. Then I saw *that man* come into view and kneel down beside him. He was showing him how to take his best shot. And then I heard Punky say, "Can I call you Daddy?"

And *that man* said, "Yes, son."

My heart burst open. I listened to that man's "yes, son" and his words ricocheted through the air, aimed directly at me.

The day of the meet I rushed in late. Mama, Rhenda, and Punky were already in the bleachers. I saw their look when they saw me. Shock. Nice. Just what I was after.

I hopped up on the racing stand. I was cutting it close. But I'd been waiting just outside the MLK Center. I knew by now Mama would know I hadn't been on the minivan that morning.

Coach came running up. He had a clipboard in his hand. I figured he was so mad at me, he hadn't even looked up. I had missed the entire week of practice sulking.

He was instructing two other swimmers who were following him like chicks follow a mother hen. He said to me, still looking at his clipboard, "Girl. You almost gave me a heart attack. You ain't got but five minutes before it's time. You ain't serious enough about this. See that man over there," he said, pointing to a gray-haired white man that stuck out among all the black people like a blue M&M. "He's here just to see you. And you out somewhere playing around. Do you hear what I'm saying to you?" he asked, finally looking up at me on the blocks.

"My God," he said, followed by a low whish of breath.

I grinned. That ought to shut him up. A whistle blew, and I saw him staring at me unable to move from the spot. Another coach grabbed him and said something to him. But he was still staring up at me.

I cut my hair off. Almost all of it. I had a short Afro. Now, I dare him to say I wasn't serious.

On the stands, I touched my new bracelet with my fingers and smiled at Betty. I gave everyone else a tiny wave. I almost fell off in the water when Malik threw me a kiss. *Man, he ain't real.*

I took some deep breaths and prepared to take *my* best shot.

When I kicked off from the wall on the last race, the 100-meter backstroke, I was bursting open. I could hear a roaring in my ears I moved through the water so fast; I tucked in my flip turns tight and at the last sprint I turned on the jets. When I came up out of the water I could hear the crowd singing, "It's all over. Da dum. It's all over." I could see Mama, Rhenda, Tomika in Rhenda's arms, Punky, Betty, Clarissa, and Phyllis and Malik jumping up and down like clowns.

Mr. Walt bent down and helped me up out of the water. He gave me a big hug. "Girl, you Olympics bound."

I felt so full. I could feel the tears as I was drying off with the monogrammed towel Clarissa and Phyllis had sent to me while I was home brooding like a pigeon.

The man, Mr. Jack Morrison, introduced himself. "You are one heck of a swimmer, young lady. Walter was right," he said, shaking his head. "You've got it. You have most definitely got it. I'm offering you a spot on my trials team this winter. Florida. Be there," he said, still shaking his head as he walked away.

Mama and the gang almost smothered me. I kept saying, "I'm wet. I'm wet."

And then I saw him.

He was standing over at the door. Just watching. Grinning and watching. I broke free of them and ran to him. I threw my arms around him the same way I'd imagined I'd do since I was a little girl. And just like in my dreams, my daddy hugged me back. I remembered Betty's words as he whispered to me.

"I love you, daughter," he said.

I could feel his tears on my cheek as he said, "The last time I held your hand I told you the same thing. You were only three years old. I loved you then and I love you now."

I squeezed my eyes shut. I had not imagined him holding my hand after all.

When he let me go, Malik was standing only an arm's length away. "Daddy, I want you to meet someone," I said, pulling Malik closer.

"We've already met," he said. "He's a fine young man, Keisha, with big dreams. I like that."

"I like it too. Yes," I said, smiling. "You know what else? I understand something now, Daddy. Me and Malik—we the future."